REVOLU<del>TIO</del>NARY
PEDAGOGY

REVOLUTIONARY PEDAGOGY

Primer for Teachers of Black Children

MOLEFI KETE ASANTE

Universal Write Publications LLC

REVOLUTIONARY PEDAGOGY: Primer for Teachers of Black Children

For information:
Submissions@UWPBooks.com
Website at www.UniversalWrite.com
IMPRINT: The Academy

Mailing/Submissions
Universal Write Publications LLC
237 Flatbush Avenue, Suite 107
Brooklyn, NY 11217-5224

ISBN-10: 0-9825327-4-1
ISBN-13: 978-0-9825327-4-4

DEDICATED TO

Jamar Ramses, Ayaana, Aion, Nova, Akila and Akira
Who will always know and teach

Contents

Preface

At the very beginning of our now centuries old sojourn in North America Africans recognized in traumatic fashion the difference between our own institutions that had been put in place for thousands of years and the new ground of enslavement and brutalization that would be implemented by Europeans as a way to teach subservience. Out of this awareness has come generation after generation the resistance to brainwashing and mental programming of our people.

It is not alarmist to say that education, as a system, has not always been our friend; indeed, the statistics of the condition of African American education suggest that education has systematically robbed black children of their motivation, creativity, cultural identity, and assertiveness. This means that children often leave school more damaged psychologically and culturally than they could have been or would have been had they remained at school. The very provocative study done by Ama Mazama and Garvey Musumunu, *African American Homeschooling*, shows that the growing numbers of African American families homeschooling their children is related to the families' belief that education in public schools, *inter alia*, demeans black children.

My concern as an educator and a consultant for the infusion of Afrocentric content into curricula has been how to teach teachers how to unlock the potential in the children sitting directly in front of them in the classroom. I have this tremendous faith in the possibilities of victories because I have never seen students who could not learn. I have seen students who it is said do not learn. I have seen students who do not score well on standardized examinations. But I also know that I have never found a student that I could not reach using pedagogy based in Afrocentric theory. What is truly remarkable is the degree to which this pedagogy can be taught and learned by thousands of teachers.

Today the principal concern in public education is the commitment to excellence of all students. If a teacher learns the mechanisms for revolutionary pedagogy all else falls into place. But as teachers we must dedicate ourselves to the task of energizing our students to be and do the best they can in order to assure their future and ours. So this book is written for teachers and teacher educators in an effort to stop the betrayal of urban children and the scapegoating of revolutionary teachers.

I have seen teachers criticized and not rewarded for their success in the classroom. These are teachers who have the ability to reach children and are often seen as "too ethnically committed" or who believe in "black history every day" or "who are culturally sensitive" to their students. These are the teachers that principals and superintendents ought to see as outliers for the kind of pedagogy that this books represents.

It is my deeply felt conviction based upon all of my studies and experiences that the teachers who utilized this revolutionary pedagogy will be among the most successful at teaching in the urban centers. However, these principles are not merely useful for the teachers of black and brown children they are useful for the teaching of any children. A teacher to teach must know something about the culture of the student to be considered an excellent teacher. Once you know your students or demonstrate an interest in knowing by reading and inquiring you will discover your own victories in the classroom. This is the theme of this book. I have addressed this book to those who have ears to hear and eyes to see the necessity of reversing the brain freeze that often accompanies, not just the students; but the teachers who are placed in urban situations and have limited knowledge about how to proceed.

Molefi Kete Asante
Molefi Kete Asante Institute for Afrocentric Studies
Temple Univeristy
Philadelphia

CHAPTER ONE

A Revolutionary Pedagogy

There is a general opinion among educators, politicians, and the public that in the United States urban education is a failure. Using various indices of the new educational regime researchers have found that schools in larger urban communities demonstrate lower scores on standardized tests, lower levels of discipline, more school absences, and often less motivation to learn. In an Executive Summary of School Conditions, the National Center for Education Statistics state "Many Americans believe that urban schools are failing to educate the students they serve. Even among people who think that schools are doing a good job overall are those who believe that in certain schools, conditions are abysmal. Their perception, fed by numerous reports and observations, is that urban students achieve less in school, attain less education, and encounter less success in the labor market later in life" (nces.ed.gov/pubs/web/96184ex.asp).

1

The NCES studied the situation and found that "Forty percent of urban students attended these high poverty schools (defined as schools with more than 40 percent of students receiving free or reduced price lunch" (nces.ed.gov/pubs/web/96184ex.asp). The NCES concludes that poverty alone could not explain all of the differences between schools when one compares one set of high poverty schools with another set. In addition to poverty one must examine issues of single parent families, school mobility, television watching time, absenteeism, pregnancy, and lack of high expectations. In my judgment most of these factors are directly related to poverty itself, whether in rural schools or urban schools, but a substantial amount of responsibility lies with teachers.

All children have the ability to learn in normal settings. Gloria Ladson-Billings, one of the most astute theorists of education, understands this more than most and that is why she has declared that few schools recognized what the students bring to the classrooms themselves. Taught, for the most part, with a pedagogy designed to maximize white cultural styles and objectives, black children, and Latino children, who comprise majorities in many large American cities are often victimized by the pedagogy and the curriculum.

There are many scapegoats offered on the altar of explanation for the quality of urban schools. Some teachers and school administrators have blamed black boys for some of the dysfunction found in urban schools. Somehow, these evaluators tend to believe, that if we can fix the inner city schools of large cities like Pittsburgh, Philadelphia, Atlanta, Chicago, New York, Los Angeles, and St. Louis, we will be on our way toward relieving the American society of a negative aspect of education. The

NEA, National Education Association, concludes "The statistics describing Black boys as more likely than their peers to be placed in special education classes, labeled mentally retarded, suspended from school, or drop out altogether is disturbing enough. But the surprising news, at once puzzling and promising, is that we actually have tools to reverse this trajectory and success stories to prove it" (*Race Against Time: Educating Black Boys* (February 2011, 2 MB, 8pp). Thus, NEA sees the statistics as disturbing but the prospects for success as promising. Any thesis about education that places the burden on the children may be shouting at obvious outliers about what is wrong with the system. Black children are not responsible for the broken urban educational system; they are often victims of it.

It is the educational system in the United States that is a failure, not the urban schools, not black boys, not the teachers, but the overall system that denies children the proper education. Taking this or that sector out of the system and holding it under a microscopic examination will not reveal the deeply flawed architecture of student and teacher disinterest in piecemeal fixes. Failure is not absolutely necessary; it must be designed, organized, and maintained to effectively mis-educate and misdirect the children it is supposed to help succeed. The information and knowledge that will aid them in deciphering the society and making life better for themselves and those around them should not be foreign but familiar.

Immediately after the Nat Turner Rebellion in Southhampton Virginia in 1831 the Virginia House of Delegates held several meetings to discuss the fear and insecurity that whites were feeling throughout the state. One delegate, Henry Berry, himself a slaveholder from the Western part of the state, spoke on behalf of the gradual elimination of slavery. It was clear to him that nothing the whites could do would completely insure their safety since the "Southhampton affair" as they called it, had shown that uneducated and illiterate Africans could rise up against them at any time. However, Henry Berry pointed out to them:

"Sir, we have, as far as possible closed every avenue by which light might enter their mind; we have only to go one step further — to extinguish the capacity to see the light, and our work would be completed; they would then be reduced to the level of the beasts of the field, and we should be safe; and I am not certain that we would not do it, if we could find out the necessary process and that under the plea of necessity. But, sir, this is impossible; and can man be in the midst of freemen, and not know what freedom is?" (Berry, "The Abolition of Slavery," Virginia House of Delegates,1831, l859).

The enslavement, of course, was a period of utter fog and even the little clarity that entered our minds was enough to convince our ancestors that they should have the same rights and privileges as those who held our people in bondage. What could have compelled whites to devise such a system but an attempt to stifle all intelligence and freedom? Numerous writers have quoted Berry out of context because they believed he was advocating a continuation of this practice but in effect he was despairing that the white slaveholders had done all they could to prevent Africans from recognizing their right to freedom and their dastardly acts had failed. He was amazed at the resilience, intelligence, and courage of enslaved Africans who kept their eyes on freedom.

Of course, after the Civil War the condition of Africans during the Reconstruction and into the 20th century was one of great desperation for education. Hundreds of whites from Northern states traveled to the South to assist blacks in reading and writing and mathematics (Anderson, 1988). The activities were important but in the end they had to be seen as another way to undermine the historical and intellectual narrative of Africans. The education was to deepen in many cases, not to relieve the burden of ignorance about self.

Education, genuine transmission of knowledge, is at the heart of transformation. I have always believed that the route to freedom leads through the *endarkening* avenues of historical and contemporary information. Self-knowledge for the African American is the first order of business in the classroom. Carter G. Woodson later discussed this in his famous book, *The Miseducation of the Negro*.

In their brilliant book, *The Afrocentric Praxis of Teaching for Freedom,* Joyce E. King and Ellen E. Swartz, connected culture to learning in a demonstrative display of both good research and good common sense about how to approach education in general and the failure problems particularly. Culture and learning are deeply intertwined in the process of socializing young people to understand their reality. These are not necessarily joined in the administration of school-based programs; administrators tend to like what they see as bringing hardware solutions to software problems. They encourage rote memory of unnecessary information if it is necessary for them to raise the scores of their children and hence be able to maintain their jobs. This is puerile and venal thinking in my judgment and serves no other purpose but to find a scapegoat for the failure of the educational philosophy that leans too heavily on testing and not enough on making good citizens.

King and Swartz contend the importance of heritage and cultural knowledge in education is fundamental, stating that "Heritage knowledge refers to group memory, a repository or heritable legacy that makes a feeling of belonging to one's people possible" (Clarke, 1994; King and Swartz, 2015, p. 29). Boaventura's abyssal thinking proponents would dismiss this profoundly important aspect of the educational process. What King and Swartz have done is to make a connection between practice and theory in the teaching of children. Of course, I favor these theorists because I think that King and Swartz are two of the most important philosophers of education but they are also practitioners in the best sense of teaching teachers. In some real ways I gained a lot for my work in revolutionary pedagogy from their idea of *teaching for freedom*.

Of course, anyone who reads me will also see that I have learned a lot from the leading anti-racist intellectual in Canada, George Sefa Dei, whose book, *Teaching Africa: Towards a Transgressive Pedagogy*, remains one of the outliers for all progressive scholars (Dei, 2010). Dei argued that history was itself a discipline that introduced and maintained colonialism. In order to overcome the tremendous hold that Eurocentric history has on African scholarship it will be necessary to introduce what he calls a transgressive pedagogy. Obviously, one can see that I upped the ante and went for a more provocative term; however, it was not just the term "revolutionary" that I went for but also the idea that we needed a pedagogy that would overturn the stereotypical notions of African people wherever we were in the world. Furthermore, I saw that what happens to us as Africans happens to Native Americans, Arabs, Jews, Mexicans, and other people in other societies. A revolutionary pedagogy shows itself as an ethical thrust into the midst of racial, cultural, economic, psychological and sectarian education.

Isolating components of the system and holding them up to criticism is a good exercise for exposure but it is not enough to bring about revolution in any category. To change the situation we will have to confront the philosophical approach to the process of transmitting information. Essentially we need a revolutionary pedagogy.

A revolutionary pedagogy will require different ways of thinking and maybe even different structural components to the school setting. If we were bold enough to look at the way children and adults learn and then implement the kind of apparatus that would capture that learning style and interest we would be looking behind the educational veil. I call this type of radical examination and suggestion a resetting of the school agenda that will liberate the teachers and the students in a school building. While this is only one step in the right direction, it remains only one step because learning styles and teaching styles operate under the regime of a symbol and cultural system that dictates what and how children will learn. Let's revolutionize the system now!

Here is what I see in a revolutionary pedagogy where everything that has to do with the school is pedagogy. I see an emphasis on the five aspects of revolutionary pedagogy *ethics, values, literacy, relationships, and reasoning*, as essential to upsetting the status quo. The first comment I will hear when I say these things is that is what schools are already doing. Of course, this is not true because we would not have racists, homophobes, narcissists and jerks coming out of the schools with declared diplomas that they have been educated. In fact, what we call "good" schools are often some of the ones where we find the least educated people. They become the hotbeds of negative thoughts about diversity, multiculturalism, and progressive projects to save the planet, Black Lives Matter protests, and fairness to Native Americans on whose land we all live. To put it mildly, we have a system in need of revolution not one that has seen revolutionary pedagogy.

If the aim of education is to teach the student how to make money then you will have to practice a pedagogy that will create the conditions for the student to learn how to make money. Such pedagogy may emphasize the big beautiful and rich business schools with famous names.

If the aim of education is to teach the student how to worship and serve God then you will have a pedagogy that will encourage students to revere that which they neither know nor understand. Such pedagogy may emphasize piety over curiosity, and subservience over creativity.

My point is that how one sees the purpose of education will dictate pedagogy. John Dewey, the legendary American educator, says, "that the general purpose of school is to transfer knowledge and prepare young people to participate in America's democratic society." Of course, this definition is woefully limited and limiting and speaks to the nativist orientation of much American thinking in the early 20th century. However, the purpose of education for the revolutionary pedagogist is to prepare students to live in an interconnected global world with personal dignity and respect for all other people as human beings with the same privileges that one seeks for oneself while preserving the earth for those who will come afterwards. This is a revolutionary point of view that incorporates the five aspects of revolutionary pedagogy.

THE FIVE ASPECTS OF REVOLUTIONARY PEDAGOGY

Relationships

We are all bound to the same human kinship. Any attempt to separate humans on the basis of physical characteristics, religious beliefs, artistic attributes, or regional origins is anti-intellectual, anti-educational, and anti-human. The core of our humanity is our relatedness first to our family and then our communities and other entities, political, religious, or artistic; but ultimately we are bound together by our humanity.

Ethics

Ethics is a consciousness of moral principles that work within the context of society and assist in the determination of what is harmful and what is useful for the community, nation, and world. Thus, all traits that support harmony, balance, order, truth, righteousness, justice, and reciprocity are at the core of protection of humanity, the universe, and self.

Values

The idea of values suggest that there are standards that have the capacity to elicit an emotional response to persons, places, themes, and other phenomena. When one knows that something is beneficial to the society we are inclined to say that the person has good values. One does not normally speak of bad values; indeed, values imply something that is good. In an interconnected world, for example, the sustaining of the world depends upon recognizing global diversity and responding to global sharing with other human beings.

Literacy

Literacy is the state of being knowledgeable of a particular category of knowledge. For example, in English the person who can understand language and express it through reading and writing is said to be literate in English. One could also be literate in music or in culture and so forth as an example of having basic knowledge upon which to build more complex information and knowledge. Scientific literacy allows students to understand and appreciate concepts such as climate change, race as an illusion, nuclear energy, and fossil fuels. A revolutionary pedagogy undertakes a profound review of E. D. Hirsch's notion of cultural literacy that heavily leans on European information and facts and not on a multicultural response to knowledge. In an arrogant and monocultural manner Hirsch promoted, and the schools systems accepted, the idea of a common core that relegated African and Asian information to a background position.

Reasoning

Reasoning is the ability to determine quantitatively and qualitatively answers based on evidence and facts. Hence, critical thinking and creative communication together allow the student to arrive at conclusions and to adequately and effectively present such results in written or oral forms. Reasoning is best when the student understands the calm reflection that is necessary to make a studied conclusion before speaking or writing.

SCHOOL ATMOSPHERICS

There is nothing wrong at all with walking into a school building and hearing some low sounds of popular music playing in the background. I would favor classical jazz but studying the various sounds of music or other sounds, perhaps, the voices of birds and the falling of water, to see how children respond might reveal a powerful ethic that school administrators have overlooked. After nearly twenty years of working as a consultant for training teachers how to teach in urban schools I have concluded that the system I created with Ama Mazama only works if the entire school system is passionately committed to educating children. It should not be necessary to say this but I have heard enough good teachers lament that they are unable to turn the educational ship around alone with their classes; it must be a district wide effort.

"Schools are often not about the children, but about testing because the bottom line is money," one teacher at an Eastern seaboard school district told me. There are lots of perceptions tied up in the knot of this statement and some may be correct and some may be wrong but one thing is certain that teacher voices the concern of scores of teachers that I have worked with over the years. It is a shocker to many teachers when they learn that some superintendents are so busy making deals with local businesses, selling off school properties, closing down schools to demonstrate to school boards how tough they can be in saving money, and paying millions of dollars for district wide contracts to a few large

testing and curriculum corporations while neglecting the programs that will have a lasting impact on the quality of children's
education long beyond testing.

The practice of revolutionary pedagogy is a fundamental tool
in the creation of a new perspective on education. One cannot take
down the entire system while it is still running just like you cannot
close out a national insurance plan when millions of people are
invested in it. Revolutionary pedagogy is an incremental process
intended to announce the complete overhaul of the educational
system. Most American schools do not need tune-ups, they must
be introduced to complete overhauls and that strategy will depend
upon bold educators.

A revolutionary pedagogy is an intellectual and emotional
commitment from the school boards and commissions to the
superintendents and principals. Whole school buy-ins will raise
the profile of any radical cultural program designed to effectively
change the school's thermostat so that principals, teachers, and
students, even cafeteria workers and maintenance people, will
know that something different is happening at the school.

Of course, there will be resistance, there is already resistance
because those teachers and administrators invested in the current
unworkable system of education will not want to change what is
comfortable for them, although the system is not working for children. It is my belief the unworkable system of education is based
on modern Western thinking that needs to be corrected in order
to allow for a revolution in pedagogy. To support my position I
am able to agree with some of the most important contemporary
writers on this subject.

For example, Boaventura de Sousa Santos has positioned the

struggle for a proper orientation to knowledge this way. He says, "Modern Western thinking is an abyssal thinking. It consists of a system of visible and invisible distinctions, the invisible ones being the foundation of the visible ones. The invisible distinctions are established through radical lines that divide social reality into two realms, the realm of "this side of the line" and the realm of :the other side of the line" (Sousa Santos, 2007). For Boaventura there is this notion that the "other side" becomes nonexistent, without reality, in abyssal thinking. Only one side or position is existent it is the side with the wealth, power, and military. Thus what is derived from the so-called nonexistent is neither relevant nor considerable; it is radically excluded, and thus beyond the abyss. The most *abysmal* idea about *abyssal* thinking is that there is no possibility of co-existence. When it is educational it becomes a rampant assertion of a right to exist without others; it is at its source arrogant, supremacist, and war-minded. Boaventura has restated the problem in a stark manner and has positioned abyssal thinking as the culprit. In this regard he is correct, it is the inheritance of a dogmatic way of thinking that must be challenged by the new revolutionary pedagogy.

However, let me caution the teachers who are ready to try this revolutionary pedagogy. Administrators tend to lag behind what is going on in the classroom; few are revolutionaries themselves because they are so busy socializing to keep their positions that they are afraid to explore what works. The best teachers in a building already know what revolutionary pedagogy is because they are doing it! They have taken the attitude that the core of revolutionary pedagogy is content. They are correct in this assessment because in the end the teacher in the classroom is the educator. They also know that they must not fear the students and indeed, must demonstrate the high moral commitment of liking the students. In most cases, administrators were educators, but to educate you have to teach and you cannot be a good teacher until the pupil has learned. All those people who say they are teachers but have never successfully educated anyone must seriously question their tag as teachers.

Christopher Emdin speaks of what he calls reality pedagogy. He sees it as an approach to teaching and learning based on youth experiences as the anchor of instruction. There is something positive in this idea but it is not sufficient. Sometimes the experiences of youth may not lead to the appreciation of the complexities and multileveled nature of the social and political context. The danger is that such an individualistic reality-based pedagogy might emphasize current situations and ideas much more than enduring values. Although one can utilize the immediate cultural styles one must be careful not to assume that these are transferable to all educational situations. One cannot base pedagogy on one individual but on panoplies of culture. This means that the pedagogy takes into consideration the entire system of history, politics, social values, and visions of a group of people. The revolutionary pedagogy motto is "Master the culture of your students before you attempt to teach them." I am aware that this is contrary to most educationalist philosophies because they think that the teacher teaches content alone, but you cannot teach content without an adequate appreciation of the culture of the students.

Revolutionary pedagogy is neither reality pedagogy nor critical pedagogy although it shares some aspects of both ideas but principally is an advance on the teaching and learning in the classroom based on an Afrocentric infusion. In most cases we speak of critical pedagogy as having to do with using concepts that are derived from critical theory in literature and sociology in the field of education. I have been dedicated to some of the key principles of critical pedagogy and in some ways have been influenced by Paulo Freire, Gloria Ladson-Billings and others who see the critical intellectual movement to open up society as necessary and powerful. My main criticism is that you cannot successfully bring something from the category of Western and American literature that is meant to buttress the status quo theorists into the classrooms in urban America and hope to have any real success. To its credit, however, critical pedagogy does bring us closer to the revolutionary idea. In fact, teaching is a political act, as critical pedagogy would contend. However, revolutionary pedagogy is not a variant of critical pedagogy; it may be considered the next phase of the movement for justice. Therefore the revolutionary pedagogist sees teaching as both a political and cultural act. Every time a teacher stands before a classroom he or she is demonstrating either his or her culture or that of the students. Knowing consciously what we are doing when we are teaching moves this act from political to cultural. When I walk into a classroom and say, "Hotep," I am consciously making a case for the value of an ancient African greeting at the same time as I am teaching the students the oldest greeting in the world. I am asserting my agency; I am being here in the world without apologizing for being. The students see and recognize themselves in this agency. Can you as a teacher learn to do this? Of course, all teachers have the ability to learn information and practices but it requires not arrogance but humility that you do not know all that you need to know to be able to teach these children.

Perhaps more than most other critical theorists, Ladson-Billings, who argued for a culturally relevant pedagogy as early as 1995 (Ladson-Billings, 1995) knew that something was not quite right with the limited notion of critical theory rooted in European dominated critiques of capitalist education alone. In fact, she argued that it was essential that many studies of student failure often located "the source of student failure in the nexus of speech and language" (Ladson-Billings, 1995, p. 467). Like the revolutionary pedagogists Ladson-Billings debunks the superficial notion "...that black people don't value education" (Ladson-Billings, 1995, p. 467). Ladson-Billings says, "A next step for positing effective pedagogical practices is a theoretical model that not only addresses student achievement but also helps students to accept and affirm their cultural identity while developing critical perspectives that challenge inequities that schools (and other institutions) perpetuate. I term this pedagogy, culturally relevant pedagogy" (Ladson-Billings, 1995, p. 469).

I have classified culturally relevant pedagogy as a variant of critical pedagogy with its emphasis on identifying *critical perspectives* that challenge inequities. This may not be entirely appropriate but it arises from the fact that revolutionary pedagogy is not merely about culture but about culture and agency and hence the idea is more about the assertion of African or Latino or Asian cultures as pedagogically important without necessary identifying critical perspectives because the assertion of our agency is itself a full critique of any kind of domination. Maulana Karenga often speaks of a reconstructive system of values that operates on the basis of "Kawaida is an ongoing synthesis of the best of African thought and practice in constant exchange with the world"(Karenga, http://www.us-organization.org/30th/ppp.html).

CRITICAL PEDAGOGY AND REVOLUTIONARY PEDAGOGY

There are some distinct differences between critical pedagogy and revolutionary pedagogy that are important to understand.

1. **Critical Pedagogy** is a philosophy of education that seeks to apply concepts of critical theory to matters of education.

Critical Pedagogy's Main Characteristics

- Uses critical theory as a base;
- Studies cultures to achieve multiculturalism;
- Advocates teaching as political act to change the attitudes of students;
- Searches for social justice to insure safety of students free of bullying;
- Believes in emancipation from oppression through critical consciousness;
- Aims to have individuals affect change through social critique and political actions.

2. **Revolutionary Pedagogy** is a philosophy of education that seeks to overturn ordinary thinking, methods, and practice of creating and delivering knowledge to children by employing Africological, Kemetological, and rhetorical techniques to reset the instructional focus for children. Africological refers to the study of African and African American history, cultures, and phenomena from the standpoint of African people as subjects. By Kemetological I refer to the origin of the African narrative in classical Egyptian, that is, Kemetic society. These ideas are especially centered on changing the way urban schools approach instruction in a radical way. How many schools even use the concept "classical Africa"?

Revolutionary Pedagogy's Main Characteristics

- Uses agency as the central concept for analysis and action; produces culturally diverse methods applicable to highly textured school settings as relates to race, gender, and class backgrounds; and realigns the core content to insure the centrality of the students' culture in the knowledge narrative whether it is scientific information or value formations based on what activates positive human responses;

- Suggests the importance of cultural justice as a way to force thinking beyond social justice so that art, music, language, robotics, and all symbol creating activities can add to the promotion of equality;

- Reaches for a robust content formula for discipline in the classroom and school building because students are awed by what they do not know but what is within their reach; and

- Aims to insure the transmission of humanizing values based on historical and social narratives that empower the students. If you set the bar high the students will leap over it!

CREATING REVOLUTIONARY PEDAGOGY

The most difficult aspect of creating a revolutionary pedagogy is the resistance on the part of the administrators and teachers who are heavily invested in the status quo. They celebrate the current system as if it is the only recourse they have. Of course, this is a mistake and a false understanding of what is required for proper education of children. Thus, for the revolutionary pedagogists the *revolution* is about overturning the status quo in the interest of educating the children. Our aim as educators is not merely to insert new ideas into the old system but to insure that the proper structures, attitudes, philosophy, and orientation are in place for us to be successful transmitters of knowledge. To this end I have identified five general themes that must be used across the board when we seek to introduce revolutionary pedagogy. I have stated them as *theses*.

Hence, a revolutionary pedagogy is based upon five fundamental theses.

1. There is no universal history with Europe at the center of it. There are only universal responses to the environment and human relations, and those responses have their own nuances and sensitivities based upon people and circumstance that seek to transmit acquired and learned behaviors to another generation.

2. In the United States, specific educational responses to the transmission of knowledge represent cultural inheritances often complicated by issues of racism, class, and gender. Separating issues so that cultural expressions, historical heritage, and personal inclinations are examined is the best way to insure revolutionary actions in education.

3. A revolutionary pedagogy begins with a proper corrective at the level of chronology as a feature of place. Without an accurate examination of time and space, it is impossible to understand the need and the nature of a revolution in the curriculum.

4. Education is the arena of ideological struggle between the status quo and the progressive forces for transformation. To overturn the status quo at the level of curriculum is to

go beyond the idea of equity and identity to the transcending of all categories that are rigidly stuck in the cementing ideas of the past in order to contest the character of a democratic society.

5. A revolutionary pedagogy must necessarily critique and reconstruct the infrastructure of contemporary education if African American, Native American, and Latino children are to be adequately educated. I believe this will become increasingly important for Asian American children as well when it becomes clear that standardized tests do not indicate adequate revolutionary education. In fact, the growing importance of optional tests for admissions for most outstanding colleges means that they are relying upon GPAs and portfolios.

On the basis of the Afrocentric paradigm introduced into the philosophical discourse on culture and identity nearly forty years ago I proposed Afrocentric education as a principal road to revolutionary pedagogy and ultimately the total transformation of American education. It was a first step but it also incorporated the idea that everything was curriculum (Asante, 1991, pp.170-172).

Afrocentricity is the process in education that seeks to locate or relocate African people and phenomena within the context of African historical and cultural agency. The key terms would have to be *centeredness, location, marginality, peripheral, location, actors, spectators, decenteredness, orientation*, and *place* (Asante, 2007; Mazama 2003). Everyone comes from somewhere and everyone is going somewhere; we are not disconnected from place, origin, or background.

I was able to use my location as an African born in a racist

American society with a history of enslavement of Africans, genocide of the native people, and the dispossession of Mexicans as an initial source for the overturn of a Eurocentric hegemony that imposed its will upon all forms of knowledge and upon all people as a conquering ideology. If the education of dispossessed people cannot produce conquest over malice and racism then that education is a failure. If white students who are in school cannot be taught the common humanity of the people of the earth then their education is essentially useless for the world they will confront.

What is the difference between Afrocentricity and Africanity? Africanity refers to the customs and styles of culture often exercised in terms of food, festivals, music, and language. Afrocentricity is a much more conscious activity, one that depends upon knowledge and will. One can practice Africanity without having any regards for transforming education or anything else; however the Afrocentrist looks at the pedagogical condition and ask, "How can we improve the agency of blacks in this or that narrative?" Since historiography is a method of writing narratives of phenomena and people, "How can one write about Africans without giving them the subject place in narratives of Africa?"

Afrocentricity is not a counterpart to Eurocentricity as it is seen in the United States and Europe. There have been several important critiques of Eurocentricity. However there is still a tendency for someone to say, "Well Afrocentricity is Eurocentricity in dark face?" Whenever I hear such a comment I know full well that the person has never read anything written by a serious scholar on Afrocentricity. While Eurocentricity tends to operate as an ethnocentric concept assuming that European ways are universal and therefore superior this is unthinkable in Afrocentricity. Indeed rather than a counterpart to this type of thinking, Afrocentricity is a definite *counterpoint*.

On the other hand , Afrocentricity is not the opposite of Eurocentricity (Asante, 1987b). In fact, Afrocentricity does not valorize itself while degrading other perspectives. Eurocentricity imposes its view as universal, making a particular historical reality the sum total, in the European's view, of the human experience (Asante, 1991). It is based on white supremacist notions which endeavor to protect white advantage in education, economics, and politics by teaching that what is white is universal, even human. On the other hand, Eurocentric instruction often devalorize what is black, African. Here the words of super teacher, Susan Goodwin, are important when she writes "Centering Black people in this discussion about educating Black children and their community brings culture, history, worldview, and ontology from the margins of importance to the foreground of required learning for teacher educators, teachers, policy makers, and the Black community" (Goodwin, August 2010, p. 1)

Furthermore, what are the implications for education if the teacher does not understand how to raise questions about the writing of history itself? Here is where the philosophy of writing, historiography, makes an entry to allow us to ask who developed the questions, who answers the questions, and what is the purpose of the questions in the first place?

APPROACHES TO REVOLUTIONARY PEDAGOGY

Afrocentricity seeks to place the African in the center of events and situations that involve African people. Why should Africans be on the periphery of their own narrative? Why should anyone dictate the narratives of knowledge or power or origin of others? Thus, the act of moving Africans to the center of their own historical narrative with all of its attendant intellectual baggage is an Afrocentric act. Using the idea of paradigm, Ama Mazama has sought to advance Afrocentricity as a transformative engine for every aspect of African life, i.e., religion, education, politics, development, and culture (Mazama, 2003).

Africology is the Afrocentric study of African phenomena from an Afrocentric point of view.

Although I believe that the Afrocentrist is closest to the revolutionary pedagogist I recognize Afrocentricity as a stepping-stone to a more holistic way of grappling with a diverse student population in a heterogeneous advanced technological society. Only the Afrocentrists and possibly the Asiocentrists Yoshitaka Miike and Jing Yin have reached the bridge across the chasm to revolutionary pedagogy because they have seen that it is not enough to "decolonize" Western education but one must act to create an ethic of revolutionary instruction. They used the so-called "fortune cookie" to show the intrusion of the West in something that was supposed to be Chinese (Yin, J., & Miike, Y, 2008, 19-43). It is impossible for Eurocentrists, especially the critical pedagogical school thinkers, to make the necessary changes because they are locked into the formula where Europe is always the teacher and others are the students. For them, critical work rarely if ever involves the criticism of Eurocentrism; it is rather a critique of liberal democracies. They do not see Europe alongside others, but rather as a neoliberal tendency that could encapsulate everybody else. Miike has explored this idea in communication theory and research and argued for a much broader perspective on communication (Miike, Y. 2007, 2).

The liberation of Eurocentrists from the need to seek hegemony will be one of the major liberations of the 21st century. One reason multiculturalism came to its end is because of the insistence on the part of some that the Eurocentric model afforded a "chance" for everyone to stand under the umbrella held by Europe. A rejection of this paternal attitude is a blow for a more revolutionary approach to culture than that we have inherited from the critical pedagogical school.

Given the overwhelmingly horrendous social policies of our society there is every reason that social justice should be a fundamental pursuit of all sectors of society. Yet it is clear that cultural justice as represented in archives of memory, symbols of success, artistic values, and dramatic genius have to be placed before our children as examples of science, art, culture, and philosophy.

I should be able to walk into any school and see an image of Imhotep, builder of the first pyramid, on the walls of the school. A series of paintings or photographs of Yenenga, Yaa Asantewaa, Hatshepsut, Amanishakete, Nandi, Queen Tiye, Nehanda, should adorn the school building and classrooms alongside the more popular images of Martin Luther King, Jr., Malcolm X, Harriet Tubman, Frederick Douglass, W. E. B. Du Bois, and Fannie Lou Hamer. Children should be surrounded by the heroes who fought for justice in all of its forms. I would like to see a corner for the astrophysicists and astronauts, the poets and novelists, the award winning dramatists, dancers and choreographers, the philosophers and educational innovators, a veritable festival of talent should stare down at the students at every turn. This is what revolutionary education looks like on the walls of a school building.

There have been many attempts to bring a more equitable

approach to education by many municipalities and several states. In New Jersey, outstanding legislators, Assemblymen William Payne and Craig A. Stanley, proposed one of the more significant movements in the nation. It was called the Amistad bill, named for the ship *Amistad* that was taken over by Sengbe and other Africans intended for slavery.

The objective of the bill was to recognize the integral part African-Americans have played at every turn in this nation's history. The Amistad Bill (A1301), which became law in 2002, directed New Jersey schools to incorporate African-American history into their social studies curriculum. This legislation also created the Amistad Commission, a 23-member body charged with ensuring that African-American history be adequately taught in the state's classrooms.

Furthermore, Assemblymen Payne and Stanley called upon the Amistad Commission to insure that there would be materials and texts that could integrate African contributions into the curriculum. They suggested that the three principal goals were:

1. To infuse the history of Africans and African-Americans into the social studies curriculum in order to provide an accurate, complete and inclusive history;
2. To ensure that New Jersey teachers are equipped to effectively teach the revised social studies core curriculum content standards; and
3. To create and coordinate workshops, seminars, institutes, memorials and events which raise public awareness about the importance of the history of African-Americans to the growth and development of American society in global context.

Leading in New Jersey in implementing the Amistad Bill was Union County Schools including towns such as Rahway and Rosedale. Almost as soon as the bill was enacted local activists in Rahway embraced the idea and pressured the superintendent to introduce a program of training teachers in African American history. What the Amistad Bill highlighted was the need to create a revolutionary pedagogy that would address the issues of culture.

Given the need to re-center historiography, the revolutionary pedagogy I suggest will seek to undermine notions of universalism and globalization that are not inclusive. All talk of mainstream without Africa or globalization that dismisses the African and Asian worlds must be abandoned. No longer can we or must we as educators be held hostages to a system of education that is meant to destroy motivation and to reduce our children to automatons.

I resent the premise upon which the current educational system is based because it assumes that something is wrong with African American children. Grounded in the doctrine of European supremacy the educational system promotes a mono-cultural insistence in education that reduces all other cultural expressions to footnotes or pop-ups.   Susan Goodwin, the Rochester, New York innovative leader of the Teacher Center, has captured one of the reasons for a lack of serious concern about the practice of pedagogy from an Afrocentric perspective. Goodwin says, "The refusal to include Afrocentric theorists as significant participants in responding to the failure of urban school districts to effectively educate Black children is a central part of the cultural denial, violence, and domination experienced by African descent communities" (Goodwin, 2010, p. 7). I believe that Goodwin has struck a chord that is central to the lack of diverse thinking about pedagogy. As I see it the Afrocentrists have raised the most fundamental questions about the educational system. They alone seem to understand that it is not enough o discuss the cultural idea without devoting extensive space and time to the question of changing the entire premise upon which we place culture. One cannot simply add Latino, African, Native American, and Asian information into the white bottle and shake it up and get what is necessary for all students. The bottle must be changed and all information must be shared from all bottles equally and poured into a new vessel. This is revolutionary; all else is nothing but domination.

Our challenges are great because while urban schools remain unchanged it is unthinkable that the achievement of low economic background children will improve regardless of their culture or racial origins. Also while the curriculum is dependent upon testing that is designed to identify students for different levels of attention the gulf between the classes will continue to grow. Giving all students proper esteem will help to elevate the thinking of the students in the classroom regardless of their class or cultural background.

CHAPTER TWO

The Problem with American Education

In June 2016 Liz Sablich wrote an article illustrating racial disparities in American education. The point that was made resonates with me: education is never a major part of the conversation of racial inequalities in the United States. Even when significant experts such as those at the Brookings Institute highlight issues that reflect disparities we are still left with a limited appreciation of the depth of racism in the system. In some respects, this is why Afrocentrists have argued for a complete revolutionary approach to the question of education. They recognize that the problem is not race necessarily but the problem is racism, deeply entrenched in thinking and buried in the soil and souls of the most liberal teachers.

The American nation has rarely dealt openly with the disenfranchisement of African Americans. From the end of the Civil

War till the top of the 21st century we have had conflicted policy about the education of black children. When the first Mohonk Conference on the Negro was held on June 4-6, 1890, A. K. Smiley quoted from a speech that had been given by former president Rutherford B. Hayes in relationship to the Conferences on the Indian, which said, "I will not attempt to say more; but so

gratified am I with what I have seen of the methods and of the spirit of this Mohonk Conference that I cannot but hope that the day may soon come when that other weaker race, not of a quarter of a million, but of six millions, shall have some such annual assembly as this to consider its condition and to aid it to rise to the full stature of true American citizenship" (Barrows, 1890). After some discussion, Hayes was elected chair of the Mohonk Conference on the Negro and among other things said, "Every Christian, will surely be persuaded that the American people have a grave and indispensable duty to perform with respect to the millions of men and women among our countrymen whose ancestors our fathers brought from Africa to be held in bondage here in America. It may be justly said in the deepest sense of the words, that we are indeed the keepers of 'our brothers in black' (Barrows, 1890). We are responsible for their presence and condition on this continent. Having deprived them of their labor liberty, and manhood, and grown rich and strong while doing it we have no excuse for neglecting them, if our selfishness prompted us to do so. But, in truth, their welfare and ours, if not one and the same, are inseparable. These millions who have been so cruelly degraded must be lifted up, or we ourselves will be dragged down." Clearly there was noted concern about the condition of millions of Africans in the American nation who did not have the same possibilities as whites. In fact, Hayes was right on in his understanding of the situation. He says, "In the Southern States are seven millions of colored people, of whom probably one-half are unable to read and write; and illiteracy in their case, we are told, means far more than ignorance of letters. It means a condition, according to a high authority, 'compounded of ignorance, superstition, shiftlessness, vulgarity, and vice'. There may be gross exaggerations in the tales we hear of the Voodoo paganism, which, under the name of religion, lurks, if it does not prevail, in the cotton and cane growing districts of the South known as the black belt" (Barrows, 1890).

Hayes had not performed well in regards to Africans when he was in the White House and there is no doubt in my mind that this gnawed at whatever sense of decency he still held after his presidency. He had come to office after a deal made with the devil, so to speak, because he had served in the Union Army and had supported the freedom of Africans from bondage yet to become president had to succumb to demands of the South to remove the soldiers from the rebellious states. In 1876, Hayes was in one of the most contentious elections in American history. He lost the official popular vote to the white racist Samuel J. Tilden because the southern states suppressed the southern black votes as well as that of the white Republicans working in the South. Hayes won a hotly contested fight in the electoral college after a congressional commission gave him twenty contested electoral votes. The result was the Compromise of 1877, in which the Southern Democrats acquiesced to Hayes's election and Hayes withdrew remaining U.S. troops protecting freed Africans and Republican office holders in the South. Ulysses S. Grant had removed the soldiers from Florida and Hayes completed the job in South Carolina and Louisiana.

When the army troops left their camps many white Republicans, the party of Lincoln people who had come to assist the Africans, also left the South. Black people felt betrayed by the white liberals who ran back to the North as soon as the protection was gone, leaving us to the vagaries, vices, and victimizations of the KKK and any other distorted minded white. Soon white Southerners dominated the governments in the Southern states.

Rutherford B. Hayes, after leaving the presidency, took on a Jimmy Carter-like stature of one seeking to do the justice that he neither had the political power nor the political will to do while he was president. Yet it must be said to his credit that he saw the problem from the same side as the evidence. A population, exploited for nearly 250 years, with untold masses who never saw a day of freedom, abused under the sun and through the night, whipped in the morning and the evening, and freed without property or proper protection, stood in the midst of an American nation built upon the backs of this people who were without education, psychological grounding in culture, or material wealth. Yet the only solution that could be proffered was the Booker T. Washington plan for educating of the hands and hearts of blacks to make better servants of the whites. Washington's philosophy was a major factor in the room with the attendees though his name does not appear on the official list of those present. Yet his dynamic presentation of black people as the willing and capable servants of the white nation, educated in the ways of the hands and hearts, was unmistakably present. In fact, this was the only solution hat made sense to the leading whites in the nation. They were not about to educate blacks to compete with whites; they could support industrial education that would make blacks better workers for white interests. Consequently, neither black children nor white children were properly educated. While blacks received inferior education in content and context whites received the doctrine of white supremacy in education because they were "better" than blacks in their minds. The whites had newer school buildings, the newest books, the most qualified teachers, and white parents figured that since their taxes were paying for the schools they "deserved" the better schools; after all, they were white. We have inherited this inequality even in an era of integration.

It should not be possible in a democratic nation for a child to attend school and after ten or twelve years leave school with attitudes like those of Dylann Roof, the Charleston, South Carolina, shooter who wanted to start a race war. What proper education would lead four young black adults to abuse a young mentally disabled white man while shouting racial epithets at him? Of course, I recognize that schools cannot do everything, but education, as its principal duty, should make a difference in how students are socialized. What are we teaching if children persist in being bigots when we have taught? What are we teaching?

This is not the end of the matter. Neither should it be possible that school readiness for black children should be eternally behind that of white children. In fact, Sean Reardon and Ximena Portilla said that between 1998 and 2010 the black-white gap in school readiness was indistinguishable from zero but where there was any perceived change there may have been several factors. They write, "There are a number of reasons to suspect that racial/ethnic and income school readiness gaps might have changed from 1998 to 2010, including changes in the income distribution (including changes in racial income disparities), changes in

parental investments in children, changes in residential segregation, changes in preschool enrollment patterns, and changes in
social policies that affect children" (Reardon and Portilla, 2016).
We have a severe problem when a certain evocative mendacity
covers every interpretation of what's wrong with the system.

I cannot accept the educational status quo in either the elementary or secondary schools in America. I can neither accept
nor appreciate the structure and scope of the curriculum in most
universities. Consequently, I am forced by circumstances to be
against the status quo, to seek its overthrow, to obliterate its racist
ethic, and to demand a new vision of education for all children.
Christopher Emdin has written an insightful book for whites
teaching in the urban areas, but this book could just as well have
been written for blacks teaching black children as well. It seems
that even black teachers, who were taught by white teachers in
school or college, have forgotten how to teach African American
children based upon the current reality. My contention is that if
you cannot teach the children from the most depressed areas of
the American cities then you should not call yourself a teacher.
Most people calling themselves teachers would have little diffi-
culty teaching children from their own socio-economic and racial
background; the real test comes when you have to teach children
that do not reflect your community or values. Lisa Delpit's dictum
on teaching other people's children is quite appropriate because it
is essential that we teach other people's children as we would teach
our own.

Black children who are punished for aggressive behavior, not
violence, are not regarded as leaders, but as troublemakers in most
academic circles. The same behavior by white students might

mark them for leadership and future potential to be successful. While some people have seen this as an economic differential, and it might be as well; I find racial animus in the way teachers, white, black, Asian, or Latino, treat African American children who demonstrate non-cognitive abilities that are said to be predictive, in some cases, of success in later life. One can examine the work of Nicholas Papageorge on this issue.

Why is it that white teachers have lower expectations for black children? I remember when I was in elementary and high school in Nashville, Tennessee, my teachers all felt that I would be successful. My teachers, with the exception of one, Mr. Brent, were all black teachers. They did not approach black children with some lower educational or academic vision than we had for ourselves. This is why the research shows that non-black teachers usually have lower academic expectations for African American students than black teachers. We also know that the more times a black student is paired with a black teacher the less likely that student is suspended from school. White teachers tend to suspend black students much more than black teachers suspend children.

Schools typically have tracking toward more advanced classes for students who live in white or Asian neighborhoods and less advanced tracking is offered to qualified students who are African American or Latino. These are decisions that are interwoven in the mythology of expectations and they significantly lower the opportunities for children in urban areas.

Needless to say that in an unequal system African American children earn diplomas and college degrees to a lesser extent than white and Asian children thus augmenting the deep trenches already left by the tracking system. With graduation rates at the high school level and the college level significantly lower than their counterparts African American and Latino students are often well on the road toward second tier standing in the society. In no society that prides itself on democracy and equal opportunity is this situation tolerable; it demands a revolutionary approach to education and to pedagogy.

CLASS AND RACE

If you show me a school in America where 75% of the children live below the poverty line I will show you a low performing school. There are no miracles here, only the terrain of class and race. Some principals know that we they are given low performing schools and asked to "turn them around" they are being set up for failure. There are a few who do not fail but for the most part any school that has 75 percent of its students coming from homes that live below the poverty level will have lower test scores. On the other hand, richer school districts do better on tests.

I am one of the first to admit that everything cannot be pinned on economics, but I still insist that economics is a major player in the arena of testing. Evidence shows that this is the case. It may be, for example, that children whose parents participate in the school program do better on tests and in behavior. So school participation is an important characteristic for school success but lack of participation is some times tied to the economic level of the parents.

So the challenge for the principal and the teacher is how to break the chain of economics so that the child will be free to learn. Here is where revolutionary pedagogy enters the picture with some ideas. You can intervene in this situation on two levels: (1) school level and (2) teacher level.

At the school level the principal must make the school a virtual home for the children so that it becomes an idealized version of the most beautiful Afrocentric home possible. In a Detroit school a principal at such a school once told me that it was hard to get the children to leave the school because they did not want to go home; the school had become home to them and they appreciated its beauty, comfort, and colors! It was cheerful, not drab. The school gave them snacks after the classes were over. They were rewarded for good behavior and had various types of awards for academics and behavior.

The teacher level is much more nuanced. There are two teacher qualities that Mario Root, a super successful school counselor at Bishop Dunn High School in Dallas, Texas, shared with me. When I was interviewing administrators about ideal teachers, Root told me that the best teachers are those who have high standards and empathy at the same time. He said that a teacher could have high standards and no empathy and that teacher would never reach the category of being an outstanding teacher. However, if a teacher only had empathy and no high standards the students would take advantage of that teacher and never be motivated to succeed. He emphasized that the outstanding teacher demonstrates high standards *and* empathy.

I did not understand school counselor Mario Root to mean that the teacher had to have high standards as in strict, rigid rules but rather high expectations of the students. Most students can see through the behavior and attitude of teachers quite easily. A teacher armed with revolutionary pedagogy sentiments will walk into the classroom with high expectations for the least of the students. I like to say to my classes, "You all have A grades today;

tomorrow depends upon you." Sometimes I also let the class know that "I believe in you and know that can get an A grade in this class. Nothing is in your way but your own efforts. I will work with you if you work with me." Students see this as an opening for them to do well and they know that if they do not do well the teacher will assist them to the limit of what is possible.

On the other hand empathy is a "feeling into the student's emotional, physical, or psychological situation." It is impossible for the teacher to know every child's situation but a teacher might be able to discover that a student has special problems by having a chat with the student when he or she is not performing well. In one high school in Philadelphia the teacher discovered that a student was getting to class late because she had to prepare breakfast for her two younger siblings because the father had to return to Hong Kong for work for several weeks. Although only a freshmen in high school this young girl was responsible for two siblings' food and dress in the mornings. For a teacher not to know these circumstances may mean that the teacher places undue stress on herself and the student by insisting that the student is a poor student. Empathy might be not simply feeling into a student's situation, but wanting so deeply the student to succeed that you show empathy. I typically ask students to tell me about their families, how are they doing, are they happy to be in class, do they have time to work at home? Establishing empathy may not change the grade but it is more likely to give a teacher a deeper insight into the situation than normal.

THE PERILS OF ADMINISTRATIVE DECISIONS

One of the worst problems faced by revolutionary pedagogy practitioners is incompetent superintendents and top administrators. They are often some of the biggest impediments to the implementation of strategies that will help students succeed. The incompetence of these administrators is not mean-spirited; it is just ignorance of how to educate children. There are several reasons for this condition. In the first place you do not have to know anything about African American culture to be a superintendent and yet when you become a leader in the larger school districts you will be confronted with the question of what to do with the lowest achieving schools in the poorer neighborhoods. Those schools are typically in the areas with the largest black populations. Nevertheless, the superintendents when offered opportunities to assist their teachers, who are mostly white, in preparing to teach the children in these low performing schools have a problem spending the money to make the necessary changes. Teachers are not well educated when it comes to the culture of the children and they rarely know how to approach children who do not have the same culture as they have as teachers. They actually need help that is not provided in any school of education that I know because one has to know both African American culture and education. Secondly, administrators are often chasing the business end of the school job so that they lose sight, if they ever had it, of providing the best education for the largest amount of students. In most districts, if the lowest achieving schools were assisted the districts would overcome more than a third of their problems with achievement. Thirdly, the school culture has a bad testing problem. This multi-billion dollar industry has seduced most school districts in the United States. Testing and evaluation children on how quickly they can answer a series of questions is now considered the best way to decide how to track students. Of course, this teaching to tests has almost nothing to do with learning and the administrators have figured out that school boards and state administrators do not want to hear anything about culture, pedagogy, only about testing scores. This is the greatest peril to African American children.

I have faced this problem in several districts including Pittsburgh and Kansas City. The Pittsburgh case is classic. The Equity and Diversity Committee, the Board of Education, and the Superintendent asked me to come speak to administrators and teachers about creating a program for insuring that students' success. The program developed by me and Ama Mazama was implemented for only six months when the district brought in another superintendent because of the retirement of the previous one. The new superintendent moved as quickly but awkwardly as possible to take down all of the programs of his predecessor, a common but fateful decision when administrations change. The fact that he had come into the district under a cloud of suspicion about fudging his resume did not help the situation. Psychologically he probably felt that he had to prove himself as a person who had higher standards than the previous administrator and therefore could not support a serious revolutionary pedagogy that asserted an Afrocentric educational training for teachers; he had to stand only for testing and evaluation on steroids. This was not only a mistake; it had no possibility of succeeding as a strategy for helping the mass of students in the district, leave alone the ones at the lowest end in the testing game. Scores only change when students are motivated to learn. Students are motivated to learn when they have teachers who are transformative in their pedagogy.

The Kansas City problem was not so much that the superintendent was not committed to doing something; it was that he had put in place no assertive Afrocentric administrators around him to insist that the schools perform the Afrocentric training as planned. The superintendent failed to oversee the principals in the two Afrocentric schools and they operated on their own with no guidance and no understanding of what it meant to be leaders of Afrocentric schools. If a principal cannot define Afrocentricity then that person has no business being around an Afrocentric school. But then again, the superintendent often gives in to the community that is demanding an Afrocentric school, because it knows this is correct, and loses sight of the revolutionary nature of this pedagogy. A true Afrocentric school has at its core revolutionary pedagogy that emphasizes the agency of African Americans in their own narrative as well as the expansion of social justice.

Overcoming the peril of weak superintendents of schools will have to be the job of the best school board members and community members, those committed to fighting for children in spite of the incompetence, especially the cultural incompetence of the superintendents.

SUCCESS DEPENDS ON LOVING THE STUDENTS' CULTURE

A long train of educators and lovers of culture precede this generation. Women particularly elevated the teaching profession with revolutionary goals. Nannie Helen Burroughs stood on the shoulders of Anna Julia Cooper and Mary Church Terrell. Like those women of the public spaces and the private strategy meetings Burroughs took to the life of education starting a National Training School to bring about an uplift in the African American community around the issues of wage earning, discipline, and making the best of difficult situations. Nannie Burroughs did not turn her dark face away from trouble; she like millions ran directly to trouble as a guardian of the race because she knew and she loved the people. White teachers who want to be successful must love the students' culture as they love their own, wanting to know more, to understand more, and to listen with an empathetic ear. Administrators who reward teachers must learn to recognize these genuine revolutionary pedagogists.

Just as we have bad administrators we have had some exceptionally gifted administrators. One of the best ever to live in the United States was the courageous and brilliant Barbara Sizemore. She was the first African American woman to head a major school district as superintendent when she was hired by Washington DC in 1973. The defining characteristic of Barbara Sizemore was her fierce determination to see black children succeed despite the negative reputation for urban schools. Nevertheless her willingness to challenge the status quo and to project the will to create raise the standards for teachers who taught black children put her in direct confrontation with the old guard of the Washington, DC elected school board. They fired Sizemore in 1975 and she went on to become a leading university administrator of education. The *Washington Post* wrote "Mrs. Sizemore assumed center stage in an arena that was wracked by social ferment, political battles and court fights during the two decades of civil rights struggles and the District's drive for home rule. The campaign for self government ended only last year with the city's first elected mayor and Council in more than a century." Calling her insubordinate, a term used frequently in reference to strong personality blacks in the 1970s the school board said essentially that they could not control her. She refused to resign and so these elected agents of the status quo had to fire her.

I have always considered Sizemore as one of the educational outliers in the sense that she was interested in raising academic achievement of African American students because she knew that African American students could learn anything any other students could learn and so she stirred controversy when she said in a speech that she had "a higher calling than educating children, and that was uplifting my race." In an interview with the *Washington Post*, she said ""I did not understand that in order to be superintendent of schools I was to give up my higher mission." Her impact was electric throughout the nation as progressives flocked to her side and made her a star in the educational arena. Perhaps her greatest champion was the professor of education at Howard University, Nancy Arnez, who claimed that Barbara Sizemore was ahead of her time. Arnez authored a case study, *The Besieged Superintendent*, which stated that Sizemore could stand up to authority and she could do things that other would not even try. Arnez told *Education Week* in 1996 that Sizemore's approach to Congress was not one of supplication but one of advocating for non-achieving students. She had made her mind up that she would do all that was in her power to transform the school district. This is a legacy of prototypical revolutionary pedagogy.

About the same time as Sizemore was making her insightful observations about the schooling of black children, Adelaide L. Sanford was championing black children as a principal in New York City. She was born in Brooklyn on November

27, 1925 and earned a B.Ed. at Brooklyn College in 1947. She received her M.Ed. degree from Wellesley College in 1950 and then taught in elementary schools until 1965 in New York. Hired as an assistant principal she was able to see the educational process up close as an administrator would see it. By 1967 she had her doctorate from Fordham University and soon became principal of Crispus Attucks School in Brooklyn where her style of leadership and powerful ethic of loving the children to motivate them to do better became the hallmark of her career. She taught students to embrace their African heritage or whatever their backgrounds happened to be. This was, but should not have been, revolutionary as a way to promote excellence and dynamic achievements. She defended her students and her faculty and soon became a household name and a national icon in the African American community of educators reaching the enviable position in the mythology of African American communities as Queen Mother. This title is bestowed informally upon women leaders who shoulder the responsibility of nurturing an entire community with their love and wisdom. It may be something unknown in other American communities but it is quite significant among African Americans. Following in the tradition of Queen Mother Moore the legendary African American woman born in Louisiana who stood up in a meeting in New Orleans where Marcus Garvey was speaking and shouted to the police and others who wanted to interrupt, "Let Garvey speak! Let Garvey speak!" She moved to Harlem and became a leader of the UNIA and other organizations including the Universal Association of Ethiopian Women and then in 1972 was given the title of Queen Mother by the Asante people of Ghana. Her battles for civil rights and systematic nationalism as well as the Garvey incident seared her name and charismatic style into African American culture. Other women would have that charisma and be accorded the title Queen Mother as well and one of the greatest is Adelaide L. Sanford who received her title before she joined the New York State Board of Regents for education. Queen Mother Sanford has been  cited by many scholars and educators for her courage and brilliance. The author Fred Monderson wrote about her in three of his books because of her solidarity with the African American community. In his book, *Ladies in the House*, Monderson celebrates a history of African women who have demonstrated an undying love of culture; Adelaide Sanford is such a woman (Monderson, 2013).

In 1986, Sanford won unanimous election to the Board of Regents of the State University of New York. As chairperson of the Regents' Committee on Low Performing Schools, she worked to shape new cultural relevant educational policies to close the gap among schools in student performance. Reflecting her community and love of African traditions and style, Sanford became known as the voice of African American students and teachers and her eloquence and impeccable African dresses brought her a larger than life reputation as fearless and courageous though never crude or rude in her statement of the issues or recommendations for solutions. Alongside serving as a regent, Dr. Sanford taught at Baruch College and Fordham University.

Many honors and awards were bestowed upon Sanford for her

work; she received the Congressional Black Caucus Foundation's humanitarian award, and distinguished alumna awards from Wellesley College and Brooklyn College. In addition, she was named one of the few *HistoryMakers*, a group of less than 10,000 African Americans who were considered world-class citizens of culture and success in all fields of science, art and education.

Sanford played an instrumental role in creating the John Henrik Clarke House in Harlem dedicated to African history, African American culture, and the promotion of the brilliant work of the late historian John Henrik Clarke. This work continues Sanford's creative approach to education, including the education of the masses of people who visit the Clarke House for lectures.

I once had the occasion of witnessing Sanford's magic as she spoke to the Rochester, New York Teachers Union, and when she had completed her brief talk, no more than fifteen minutes I was moved to ask permission to say a few words. When Susan Goodwin, the moderator said that I could speak. I remember speaking extemporaneously and saying, "What words can convey the intellect, grace, and beauty of a natural born queen? I only know that when one is in Adelaide's presence with her large invit-ing smile that embraces her children, her people, it is as if one is in the presence of the origin of awe. So today, to be warmed by her sun is magnificent because her knowledge of education and love of inner city children suggest radiance beyond the ordinary." I took my seat to the applause of the audience who had shared in my own sentiments. We had seen up close the dance of a Master Teacher and felt blessed by her steady sense of purpose and eternal optimism about the future of education.

Adelaide Sanford's trip to Vicksburg, Mississippi, as a small child had a profound impact on her. After her mother's car had been forced off the road and into a ditch, Sanford's mother soon found herself fending off prosecution from a racist judge and enduring a surgical procedure for an injury without anesthesia. Talking to Adelaide Sanford about this incident one can see that she developed an intense hatred of racism and inequality and knew that obstacles placed in the way of black children often went right back to racist attitudes that saw black children as less than white children. She vowed to break the back of this sought of racism in education wherever she could. Her unyielding belief in the capacity of black children to succeed was often met with skepticism and roadblocks. Her efforts to gain quality education facilities for black children extended to workers as well. After prolonged confrontations with New York Mayor Robert Wagner, Dr. Sanford led the effort to ensure black laborers were able to work on school construction projects throughout the city of New York. After all what we discovered was that one could not separate educational equity from general equity; what confronted teachers and students in the educational sector were problems similar to the ones found in other sectors.

All people, in every country and of every nation, have identified individuals who deserve to be celebrated and praised for the work that they are doing and have done. The names of Harriet Tubman, Marcus Garvey, Zumbi, Queen Tiye, Nehanda, Toussaint L'Ouverture, Dessalines, Fannie Lou Hamer, Abdias Nascimento, Nat Turner, Yanga, and a thousand others sing out from the panoply of heaven that we are witnesses to a profound living giant who walks among us.

Adelaide Sanford came into the world as it announced her as

a child of Africa. Her resistance to oppression of our children; her incredible defense of African American culture as a teacher, a principal, and while sitting on the New York Board of Regents for Education and her masterful teaching techniques have honored the fighting educators beyond words.

Haki and Safisha Madhubuti opened one of the first African American networks of charter schools in 1998. The network, under the name Betty Shabazz International Charter Schools, includes Betty Shabazz Academy (grades K-8), Barbara A. Sizemore Academy (grades K-8) and the DuSable Leadership Academy (grades 9-12). Betty Shabazz was named for the wife of Malcolm X and DuSable was named for the African, probably of Haitian origin, who was the first settler in Chicago. Barbara Sizemore Academy was named after the former Washington school superintendent, the first African-American woman to lead a major school system The network of schools consistently produced exemplary, high achieving students with a profoundly deep understanding of and appreciation for their cultural identity, and a desire to make the community better. So the schools gained reputations for instilling pride, motivation, and a sense of purpose in the children. However, like other Afrocentric charter schools the famed Chicago schools have found it difficult to teach the children to score well on standardized tests. In fact, Martell Teasley wrote in the *Journal of African American Studies* in January 2016 that the two dozen Afrocentric charters he examined fell short of national testing standards. Teasley said that he supported the concept and mission of the schools, but that they needed to prepare all the students for standardized tests. Without that, he said, African-centered schools will fail to earn mainstream legitimacy and will be soft targets for school boards looking to make budget cuts (Teasley, 2016).

The rise of consciousness during the 1960s was partly ushered in by the poet Don L. Lee who became Haki Madhubuti and Carol Lee, who became Safisha Madhubuti. After founding Third World Press and the Institute for Positive Education, Carol D. Lee got a doctorate and became a professor of education and social policy at Northwestern University. Haki, already a famous poet, became an administrator and publisher. They have become a legendary couple in the movement for Afrocentric schools.

Freya A. Rivers is a direct intellectual and educational descendant of Barbara Sizemore and a consistent colleague of Adelaide Sanford's style of determination but with a more robust philosophical perspective on what has to be done for African American children. Sizemore's attitude and general sense of what was wrong with the system were exceptionally astute, but Rivers took the issue to another level and proposed to create the type of school that was necessary to overcome the narratives of failure. Thus when she created Sankofa Shule in Lansing, Michigan, she was seeking to introduce an Afrocentric infusion into a charter school. After leaving Sankofa Shule, Rivers went on to establish one of the most important Afrocentric infusion consulting groups in the nation, the Genius Academy, with Julian Brooks, Lamailede Assata Moore, Shariba Rivers, and Angie Hawkins-Rivers. Sankofa Shule was called an "Educational Powerhouse" by *U.S. News and World Report* because Freya Rivers, as superintendent and founder, refused to believe the myths about black students. She had received her B.S. from Louisiana State University, an M.Ed. from Southern University and the doctorate from Vanderbilt

University. Freya Rivers overlaid every aspect of the Sankofa Shule with assertive African cultural images, motifs, cultural ideas, and values.

It is tempting to speak of Freya Rivers as a person with an enormous, more than thirty five years of educational experience, and use this as a justification for her success, but this is only half correct. Many educators work in the field for thirty, forty, and even fifty years without ever understanding the significance of a centered education for students. This is why I say that Freya Rivers had an active intellectual curiosity about the educational system itself that allowed her to make a powerful demonstration of what African American students could achieve. I was her history and cultural consultant when she took forty African American elementary children to Egypt to see the pyramids built by Africans in Africa! We took them to the villages of the contemporary black Egyptians, the descendants of the builders of the temples and tombs, and saw how inspired these students were and how reciprocal was the feeling of the Egyptians. Young children who could read Japanese, kiSwahili, and Middle Egyptian stunned the elders in Egypt and those along as chaperones. It is rare that we see change agents as brilliant as Freya Rivers whose exhibition of teaching with and for excellence inspired a generation of educators. In effect, Freya Anderson Rivers found her voice in education because of the courage of Dr. Dupuy H. Anderson who was a local human rights fighter in Baton Rouge, Louisiana. Anderson, Rivers' father, had sent her to school in Baton Rouge in the 1950s as a part of the grand attack on segregated schools in the South. In her memoir, *Swallowed Tears,* Rivers points to her father as one of the central influences on her life because he persisted in creating change in spite of threats on his life. This experience has steeled Freya Anderson Rivers against all obstacles to properly educating African American students.

The revolutionary pedagogist often appears in the classroom unbeknownst to a school superintendent but who is well known to a principal and the students in her classroom. This was the case with Christine Thomas Wiggins who was a teacher at Martin Luther King High School and Morris E. Leeds Middle School in Philadelphia for 12 years. During that time Christine Wiggins proved to be one of the most outstanding teachers in her schools. At Leeds she made a major contribution to the infusion of African American content in the lesson plans of the school. Colleague teachers were impressed with Wiggins' dedication to the idea that black children needed to have confirmation of their intellectual capacity based upon their history and cultural legacy. This was the essence of the Afrocentric idea.

Leaving the role of teacher in 1998 Christine Wiggins founded her own charter school, Imhotep Charter School in Philadelphia, with an emphasis on technology and mathematics. Naming the school Imhotep as a sign of respect for the first multidimensional genius in the African world, Imhotep, who built the first pyramid and established medicine as a science in the Nile Valley.

Numerous associations and organizations have recognized Wiggins for her brilliance and foundational knowledge about culturally relevant education. She has received awards from the National Council of Negro Women, the Cheikh Anta Diop International Conference, and the City of Philadelphia Mayor's Office.

Using the Seven Principles, the Nguzo Saba, and the concept of Maat, as a foundation Wiggins built her 600-student school on solid ideas from African culture. The seven principles have become a core part of any attempt to create revolutionary pedagogy. Established in the 1960s as keys to Kawaida philosophy as taught by the cultural philosopher Maulana Karenga, the Nguzo Saba because instruments for instruction and discipline in many schools (Karenga, 1997). The principles in kiSwahili and English are: Umoja, unity; Kujichagulia, self-determination; Ujima, collective work and responsibility; Ujamaa, cooperative economics; Nia, purpose; Kuumba, creativity; and Imani, faith (Karenga, 1997). Basing many of her instructive techniques on these principles Mama Chris created an atmosphere that was structured, definitive, and disciplined. However, Wiggins' school ran into trouble with its board after twelve years of solid work. In effect, members of the board who did not understand Afrocentricity or the ideas behind passionate love and nurturing of students in a revolutionary manner sought to rein in the school's idealistic objectives. Ultimately, the founder of the school had to leave her creation that had become a institutions without the principles she had fought to insure. Wiggins is a heroic figure although the process and the project of the school introduced the tragedy of misguided and inappropriate leadership. Revolutionary pedagogy is not without its challenges, internal and external, but it is truly on the right side of history. Teachers have joined in this movement even without administration support but where they have the support of principals they will continue to grow and to combat ignorance.

Priscilla Agbeo speaks about her experiences with revolutionary teachers at a Chicago school led by Assata Moore. According to Agbeo, when she needed the courage to lead Moore gave her the opportunity to teach. Indeed, she writes that Lamailede Assata Moore, the head of the school, made her feel like "I got this." Being taught through modeling the ideas of self-identity and self love, Abgeo demonstrated an intense emotional attachment to children learning.

Also the instructional counselor Shariba Rivers, was the "epitome of divine Black womanhood for me" according to Agbeo. She said that the "grace, intelligence, confidence, and overall energy moved me to carry myself like she did." There was something singularly important about the way Shariba carried herself as a teacher and counselor. This radiance, that Agbeo sees in Rivers, represents the kind of image that is ordinarily conveyed by those who love to teach.

CHAPTER THREE

Situating A Revolutionary Pedagogy

Carter G. Woodson's *The Mis-education of the Negro* established the principles that influenced both the Afrocentric and the revolutionary pedagogy of this era (Woodson, 2013). First published in the 1933, Woodson's classic book revealed the fundamental problems with the education of the African person in America to be the lack of knowledge of self. Since this is the first knowledge that is required to be sane and stable, the lack of it meant that African Americans were educated against themselves. Indeed as Woodson understood the African American was educated to love the traditions and ideas of other people and cultures and consequently we were only attached to the fringes of European culture.

Carter G. Woodson recognized that the African American student could not have a substantive and meaningful life within the context of American society. Even during the nadir in race relations Woodson did not reject American nationality or citizenship; he simply resolved to teach African Americans who had not been long out of enslavement how to shield against the most treacherous forms of cultural and social injustice (Woodson, 2013). Woodson understood the peculiar relationship the African person had to the American nation but he also knew that for the African to assume that he or she was in the same position as the European *vis-a-vis* the realities of America would mean spiritual, psychological and cultural death.

Education for Woodson was at the top of the ladder for renewal and revolution. He saw that the elite class of educated blacks had betrayed the community by running after European culture and ideas more than recovering and reconstructing their own. He was disappointed at the African American colleges because they were so deeply entrenched in the European ideology of white superiority that they simply became imitated of what had oppressed Africans.

Therefore, my principal impetus for development of an Afrocentric response to the phenomenon of *dislocation,* was Carter Woodson's alert recognition, nearly ninety years ago, that there was something severely wrong with the way African Americans were being educated. Woodson could not understand why we could not be taught to appreciate and love our own culture first. It troubled him that the black middle class had abandoned the love of African culture.

Afrocentricity seeks to respond to the dislocation of the African person by providing philosophical and theoretical guidelines and criteria that are centered in the person's perception of reality. A revolutionary pedagogy that would lift others urges Native Americans,

Mexican Americans, Asian Americans and others who see their cultures underrepresented and misrepresented in the system of education to join the transformation of the system. Yet the African American community cannot and must not wait to begin the immediate implementation of principles of a revolutionary pedagogy wherever we can. Our children are under severe stress and are psychologically harmed by the education that they are receiving. In the book by Ama Mazama and Garvey Musumunu, *African Americans and Homeschooling*, the authors pointed out that most African Americans who home school their children do so because of the fear of racism in the schools (Mazama and Musumunu, 2014). This is not merely a fear of racist language against the students but racist attitudes and behaviors that model disdain for the incredible history of resistance and creativity in the black world.

There can be nothing wrong with students viewing phenomena from the perspective of the African person. In education it means that one provides students' the opportunity to begin study of the world, its people, concepts, and history from the point of view of the African child's heritage. Thus, the African American child is not an object but a subject, not someone who is only the descendant of enslaved persons but the descendant of those who resisted enslavement even to the end of their lives. No discipline of knowledge is alien to the African person from this perspective. Whether the subject is biology, medicine, literature, architecture, mathematics, or social studies, the African student is centered in the reality of that discipline so that he or she is not seen as "having to go get it" but rather being a part of it. Peppered throughout the subject matter in the curriculum are the gems of inventive knowledge and intelligence.

Certainly George Washington Carver who occupies a central place in the emergence of America's agricultural revolution in the 20th century must be seen as a model of brilliance and resolute determination to bring into existence an entire community of agrarian innovators. At Tuskegee Institute in Alabama he dedicated his life to the laboratory in one of the great achievements of modern American education planting seeds of genius throughout the world to the extent that the Soviet Union under Lenin requested that he become the leader of their agricultural ministry. The fact of the matter is that he was not alone in African Americans in science. Indeed he was no more than a descendant of Benjamin Banneker who completed the work of L'Enfant in laying out the District of Colombia and giving the United States one of its first wooden clocks. I cite Carver and link him to Banneker as we should cite the continuity of this spirit of inventiveness in the African people. All revolutionary pedagogists must hunt down the strands of genius that can become fixtures in the way we think about any subject. There is nothing that has been achieved in any field that has not seen some African person engaged in it or something cognate to it.

A revolutionary pedagogy is the quest for student centricity and it encourages the locating of students within the context of their own cultural referent as a way of strengthening them in a multilayered universe where they are not on the periphery but share in the center of the thematic narrative. Thus, this applies to students from any culture. The most productive method of teaching a student is to place the student within the context of knowledge (Dei, 2010, p xxvi). For the white student in America, this goes without saying because almost all of the experiences discussed in classes are from the standpoint of white history. This is as true for a discussion of the American Revolution as it is for a discussion of Dante's *Inferno.* Yet few students in high school have ever read a short story by John A. Williams, Alice Walker, or Paul Laurence Dunbar, three of the most gifted individuals ever to write in this country. What does this say about the absolute dismissal of black cultural referents in the classroom? How does this play out in the lives of black children? You can ask the same about the Vietnamese, Latino, or Filipino student in the classroom.

I tend to believe that the vanguard people for changing America for the better have been the descendants of the enslavement because we came from such depths of depravity and experienced the most brutal of all evils in the society without being completely decimated as happened to so many Native Americans. The dominant society has a way of turning every event on its head so that schooling makes the victims the perpetrators of their own abuse; creates ideas of white generosity in the midst of white enmity toward a struggling people; and refuses to admit white guilt in the genocide of the Native Americans and the enslavement of the Africans. Thus, even a discussion of the European Slave Trade concentrates on what the whites were doing to Africans instead of the resistance of the Africans. In such a world, the African student is always acted upon but seldom showed to be an actor. A revolutionary pedagogy must be practiced in such a way that students from various cultures see themselves as participating in the flow of information and knowledge as well as in the resistance to all forms of human denials and negations.

Despite the powerful work that James A. Banks did in reasserting the five dimensions of multiculturalism he faced resistance to this simple idea. Banks asked for five things: content integration, knowledge construction, equity pedagogy, prejudice reduction, and an empowering school culture (Banks, 2007). Revolutionary pedagogy incorporates all of the dimensions of multiculturalism but adds a radical twist to the concept by insisting that white culture be seen as one of the cultures. It is not enough, for example, to speak of knowledge construction without giving some space for European descended children in this process. After all, we all do construct knowledge, but what must be insured is that 'white" knowledge does not assume a position of superiority over that of other cultures. In the same vein, when Banks speaks of "equity pedagogy" and mean by this term that teachers should adjust their teaching techniques to accommodate all cultures and genders he is asserting a basic tenet of revolutionary pedagogy. The reason I have not simply adopted the term equity pedagogy is because revolutionary pedagogy demands much more than the teacher adopting a particular style; it demands that the teacher abandon certain ways of thinking about race and gender. Nevertheless, it is important to affirm the work done by Banks to redirect our thinking about multiculturalism.

In a multicultural nation the best way to educate the children is by using genuine multicultural perspectives based on equity for everyone, including whites. I have always seen multiculturalism as the quality of respecting and accepting a variety of cultural perspectives in education without hierarchy. The fact that European culture is the majority culture in the United States is no reason for it to be imposed as universal. Education, to have integrity, must begin with the proposition that all humans have contributed to the national discourse on transforming schools.

THREE PROPOSITIONS FOR REVOLUTIONARY PEDAGOGY

I suggest three propositions for a revolutionary pedagogy based on Afrocentric infusion.

1. Education is fundamentally a social phenomenon; it consists in socializing children. Of course, pedagogy is a political act in the sense that it allows the teacher to assume that he or she knows best what and how to teach.

2. To send a child to school is to prepare the child for being part of a social group. If the teacher assumes that the child cannot become a part of the preferred social group then the child is often prepared for different paths and the discourse becomes what can we do with these children.

3. Societies develop schools suitable to the societies. Hence, a white supremacist system develops white supremacist education.

The goal of the revolutionary pedagogist is to penetrate the curtain of ignorance with the sharpest analysis of the smothering fabric of defeat covering or hiding the genius of children. Let the children breathe in the air of African and African American cultural narratives that all good educators have seen as positive weapons against anomie. In late 2016 Nigel Roberts wrote a powerful piece for *NewsOne* on what he called "10 Unsung Heroes of Education." I was humbled to be a part of the list that included Fanny Jackson Coppin, Marva Collins, Edmund Gordon, William Leo Hansberry, Charles H. Houston, Kelly Miller, Frederick Douglas Patterson, Mary Jane Patterson, and Inez Beverly Prosser. When you examine the lives of the great educators one thing that leaps out quickly is that they loved teaching black students, and by

extension, all students. They had and have a belief in the possibility of changing lives. They are obsessed with winning the student
over and will set up a contest between themselves and the student
to make a difference. So one does not have to agree with all of
the ideological positions taken by these educators to see that they
have been on the road to discovering greatness. Marva Collins
started a school in her home in Chicago in 1975 because she knew
black students could learn. Collins was neither an Afrocentrist
nor a revolutionary pedagogist; she was a committed teacher who
trained more than a thousand teachers.

Although I disagree with her method I understand full well
what she was fighting against. Collins wanted to prove to the
naysayers that our children could master any of the histories,
literatures, and science subjects that whites could master, so her
program was steeped in classical European knowledge. What
did she prove? She showed conclusively that black children
could learn anything any other children can learn. However, I
would have been more excited had she followed the pattern of
the Afrocentric educators like Barbara Sizemore, Wade Nobles,
Freya Rivers, and Asa Hilliard. Not only would the students have
learned, as Freya Rivers demonstrated, they would have excelled.
Nevertheless, one cannot forget that Marva Collins attempted to
demonstrate that black children were quite brilliant when it came
to classroom learning.

We also have the testimonies about the clear insights and richly
textured curriculum and resources originating with Maulana
Karenga and Limbiko Tembo, the leader of the African American
Cultural Center's School, in Los Angeles. Renamed for her as the
Limbiko Tembo school for African American Culture the school

is an educational institute dedicated to inspiring children to reach for excellence. Accordingly, it stresses the responsibility for children to have a social consciousness, a respect for human diversity, and community service. Limbiko Tembo was teacher, vice principal and principal from 1979 to 2009. In a eulogy for her, Karenga wrote in the *Los Angeles Sentinel*,

"We know and honor you first as *Mwalimu*, teacher, speaker of the clear and mind-opening word, instructor in lessons of life and living, careful cultivator of the love for learning; rightfully attentive to the culture, the dignity and respect-demands of everyone; daring to give special rank and relevance even to an infant; Seba, moral teacher of the sacred word, tireless teacher of the good, the right and the possible and continuous student of the ancient teachings for insight, inspiration and ever-deeper understandings" (Karenga, June 25, 2009). The special motto of Seba Limbiko Tembo and others associated with the Limbiko Tembo School is "to do that which is of value is for eternity" (Karenga, 1984). Among the administrators and teachers of this school are Principal Mwalimu Thanayi Karenga, Vice Principal Mwalimu Thema Rikondja, Mwalimu Seba Chimbuko Tembo, Mwalimu Sanifu Adetona, Mwalimu Kojo Rikondja, and Mwalimu Hasani Soto. They are bound to teach the best values of African culture and make a concentrated effort to insure that students recognize themselves as Africans with the right to be full participants of all knowledge. However, the first rule is to know who you are. The Limbiko Tembo School operates fundamentally as a Saturday School for children ages 3-11. It stresses African American history and culture.

One of the key educators to be passionate about the betrayal of black boys was Jawanza Kunjufu who took it upon himself to study the rate and intensity of schools sending black boys to special education and then decided to write several important books on the subject. As early as 1985 Kunjufu wrote *Countering the Conspiracy to Destroy Black Boys, Volume 1.* There would be three more volumes and then he would write the book, *Keeping Black Boys Out of Special Education,* as an array of powerful indictments against a system that sought to blame everything wrong in the schools on the assertiveness of black boys.

The escape hatch for African Americans has to be the re-orienting of the educational enterprise by raising the same questions that Woodson posed more than fifty years ago. One raises the questions as an assertive act by seeking in every situation the appropriate centrality of the African person (Asante, 1991). Thus, the person of African descent should naturally be centered in his or her historical experiences as an African. In education it means that we do not marginalize children by placing them in positions that causes them to question their own self-worth because their story is seldom told. The little African American child who sits in a classroom and is made to accept as heroes and heroines individuals who defamed her people during their lifetimes is being actively de-centered, marginalized, and made a non-person, one whose aim in life might be someday to attempt to "shed her blackness: as a badge of inferiority rather than to claim it as an honor for those who fought for us.. Afrocentricity places the child in her proper historical setting.

Some African writers, professors, and artists rush to deny their "blackness" because they believe that to exist, as a black person is not to exist as a human being. These are the individuals Carter Woodson said preferred European art and languages to African art and languages, who believed that what was of European origin was inherently better than what their own people had produced. Eurocentric curricula produce such aberrations in the African person. A truly educated person would view both African and European education as significant and useful, indeed, the white person who was educated in such a system could no longer assume superiority based upon false education.

THE REVOLUTIONARY CHALLENGE

The most revolutionary challenge to the ideology of white supremacy in education during the last decade is the Afrocentric idea. No other theoretical position stated by African Americans has ever captured the imagination of such a wide range of scholars and students of history, sociology, communication, anthropology, and psychology.

Three Critical Challenges to White Supremacist Teachings

Afrocentricity poses a revolutionary challenge to white supremacist education in three critical ways discussed below:

1. It questions the imposition of the white supremacist view as universal history: classical, continental, explorers, etc. (Asante, 1990).
2. It assaults ignorance by demonstrating the indefensibility of the supporting racist theories about multiculturalism.
3. It radically projects a humanistic and pluralistic viewpoint (revolutionary pedagogy) by articulating Afrocentricity as a valid, non-hegemonic perspective in this regard while encouraging other cultures to do the same so that Europe is not above others but seen as proper within its own context.

Afrocentricity relates to revolutionary pedagogy as an essential step on the ladder to operationalizing the concept. Inasmuch as revolutionary pedagogy is about deconstructing and disrupting the status quo no other philosophical paradigm has adequately started that process. Afrocentric education centers the child in history and culture, rather than outside of it. It is therefore on the road to the paradigmatic state which is revolutionary. How alien must an African American child feel in those cases where the information being presented makes the child feel like an outsider? In most classrooms, whites are located in the center perspective position. Whatever the subject, the African person is on the outside. Nevertheless, as Marva Collins has demonstrated the black child with dedicated and committed teachers who believe in the children can master that information regardless to its dislocating effect. Even if we wanted a truly multicultural education that also must initially be based on an Afrocentric initiative, otherwise the African American child will continue to be lost in the European framework. While all children can learn the most valuable role the teacher can play, that is, the most ethical is to begin with self identity.

AFROCENTRICITY AND HISTORY

A few years before his death Arthur Schlesinger and others formed what they called a "Committee for the Defense of History." But history needs no defense, only lies, untruths, inaccurate information need defending. This committee was nothing more than an attempt to buttress the crumbling pillars of a white supremacist system that has maintained its legitimacy by concealing its motives behind the cloak of American neo-liberalism. Such a movement is in the same spirit and tradition as Allan Bloom's *Closing of the American Mind* and E. D. Hirsch's *Cultural Literacy*; both books were placed in the service of the white hegemony in education, particularly in curriculum and Hirsch made millions of dollars when his work was considered by conservative politicians as useful for the Common Core in public schools

Cheikh Anta Diop, the late great scholar, told me in Dakar, Senegal, in December, 1980, "African history and Africa need no defense." Thus, when I heard that there were white scholars, joined by some blacks, who thought it was necessary to defend history, I knew that they must have had a lot of shoring up to perform. But perhaps in a discussion of the curriculum which would open it up in a profound way it was inevitable that the closets of bigotry would reveal various attempts to defend white privilege in the curriculum as it had often been defended in the society. This was a predictable challenge to the thrust for pluralism. Their attempt is no more than a defense of the received interpretations of a racist history, written pre-eminently from a hegemonic, white supremacist perspective. Those who argue against the Africa-centered or Afrocentric perspective often cloth their arguments in false categories and fake terms (Keto, 1990).

Afrocentric education is not *against* history: it is *for* history, correct, accurate history. If it is against anything, it is against marginalizing African American children, Latino children, Asian American, Native American children-a true revolutionary pedagogy will be different from a racist education, that is, a white supremacist education.

Frankly, perhaps the most unsettling aspect of revolutionary pedagogy for many whites and some African Americans is that its narrative power and its analytical power is derived from Afrocentric authors. Of course, as we know some white writers and many Asians have written outside of the Western box. I am thinking particularly of the works by C. K. Raju and Ana Monteiro Ferreira (Raju, 2012; Ferreira, 2015). Raju's push to decolonize the universities around the world and Ferreira's critique of modernism and postmodernism may represent aspects of this new revolutionary pedagogy. White Americans and Europeans have always had charge of major ideas in the American academy: *deconstruction, gestalt psychology, marxism, structuralism, early childhood education, etc.*, have been articulated, elaborated upon, and developed by white scholars. On the other hand, Afrocentricity is the product of mainly African and African American scholars such as Ama Mazama, Wade Nobles, Asa Hilliard, Maulana Karenga, C. T. Keto. On the African continent the works of Simphiwe Sesanti, Vusi Gumede, and offer new insights into the discourse around revolutionary pedagogy. Indeed there are increasing numbers of young African American scholars and some young white scholars, influenced by philosophers like Frantz Fanon and Lewis Gordon, who have begun to write in the revolutionary vein.

Fanon is a patron saint of confrontation of negativity and hence he exists as someone to profoundly teach us how to approach pedagogy in a world of conflicts.

To understand fully the essence of Frantz Fanon for education, it is necessary to have an idea of the world in which he lived. Without a proper location of his place in the world we are unaware of the motives that generate a statement like "I came into the world imbued with the will to find a meaning in things, my spirit filled with the desire to attain to the source of the world, and

then I found that I was an object in the midst of other objects."
(Fanon, 1967, p. 109.) Here Fanon is expressing himself as so
many other blacks have expressed themselves in the throes of self-
discovery while sitting in a classroom listening to the report of
another white intellectual. Fanon was conscious of the white gaze
as every black child in a classroom with a majority of white students must feel, the hegemonic thinking of white individuals or
teachers that pictured him and others like him as objects on the
periphery of humanity and knowledge. This observation was part
of his salvation, if indeed, we can ever say that Fanon saw clearly
enough to be saved. "Mama, the nigger is going to eat me up"
Fanon has the little white boy crying to his mother in "The Fact of
Blackness". In this facet of his understanding, Fanon knows that he
is a subject although he is quick to say that he is an object among
other objects, but alas, this is the case only in hegemonic societies
where whites see blacks only as objects whether in schools or out
of schools. Fanon is located in the engine of agency; he reacts not
like an object but like one fully in control of his will.

The idea of agency has two important parts; the spirited will to
save oneself and others and the acceptance of the critical responsibility that comes with agency. The first part is almost automatic
once a person gains consciousness of the historical crime that
has been committed against Africans and other systematically
oppressed people. It is almost a reaction of personal safety and
security. It is as if the person says "I cannot allow the oppressor
to stand in the way of my will; if necessary I *will* do everything in
my power to eliminate oppression even if it means being violent
against the oppressor. In schools this is the student who *refuses* to
learn or *refuses* to engage in the classroom as an act of resistance.

I call this a spirited will because it is not simply knowledge or consciousness but an active participation in one's freedom. It is the spirit manifest in Nat Turner or Harriet Tubman or Fannie Lou Hamer. The second part of agency carries a very high ethical responsibility; that is what I mean when I call it a critical responsibility. Fanon understood that we were the authors of our destiny but that each human being had to make a series of decisive breaks in order to be truly human. When I am able to see clearly enough with the consciousness that I have gained I will be able to understand that it is only when I have centered myself in my own historical and existential reality that I will be able to make the proper moral judgment of myself and my fellows. If, in my mind, I am in the margins of human history or on the fringes of historical reality I will never be able to think of myself as properly human, meaning properly responsible, and hence I will forever be a victim. Of course, I cannot be held accountable for my actions either because I am an object, one that might be fabricated as a commodity and sold on television or the web as the black body. In education I become a number a test score, or a statistic, but never the subject of my own narrative and those who read me or listen to me only do so out of a sense of superiority to me. I am therefore nothing more than a commodity in the classroom. How much money can the school get from the federal government?

In many ways Fanon speaks clearly and profoundly to me personally because I have refused to surrender my rage, a significantly human part of me, in the face of patriarchy, prejudice, homophobia, sexism, white privilege, and capitalist greed. Since I have never seen myself as, nor do I seek to become a Public Intellectual, I cannot be seduced by material trinkets. As an Activist Intellectual, however, I intend to pursue to the greatest extent possible the overthrow of all forms of academic tyranny and intellectual terror against black students. As an African I see this intention as a part of my challenge to enthrone a kingdom of Maat with its attendant ideas of justice, righteousness, harmony, balance, truth, order, and reciprocity. What this really means to me, a revolutionary pedagogist, is that we must work to bring into existence a world that Fanon would have sought.

The world made by Fanon is one quite familiar by now to the revolutionary pedagogists who seek to establish rationality at the center of the academic being. What can be any greater for a person than to be seen as a participant in the drama of life rather than a spectator to dramas being played out by others? To be inside the drama, acting and performing with intelligence and rationality, is to be at the center of the cosmos, as far as we know the cosmos. I mean we do not know everything, and that was even obvious to the brilliant Fanon, but we know enough to believe that those who have been pushed off of their own terms, alienated as it were from their own histories, names, values, and traditions cannot act rationally without being re-centered. To liberate one's self is both to break through to agency and to refuse to allow others, whatever their status, to violate you. For me it is this realization at the moment of decision that marks the most powerful identification of personal and collective liberation with genuine education.

The domination of others is a variety of colonialism, even if on a personal scale; the resistance to domination is a variety of anti-colonialism. Like Fanon the revolutionary pedagogist sees domination whether physical or linguistic or in any other form as a challenge for a regimen of resistance. Nothing should ever force us to allow the codification of domination or any other Western modernist notion of controlling space and place to subvert our liberation. In effect, you must be ready to fight against all types of conformist rhetoric, action or education.

SUPPRESSION AND DISTORTION

African American scholars trained in the best universities and with some of the most impressive credentials have now emerged with ideas about how to change the curriculum Afrocentrically. The forces of resistance to this transformation began to assemble around their wagons almost as quickly as the word was given that education had to treat each child equally. The attempt was to discredit the intellectual and philosophical movement because white scholars at the major universities did not start it and have not discovered how to articulate it. Yet, even without the ability to quote a single word on the theory, they write articles against Afrocentricity often criticizing it as a separatist movement, a further indication of their lack of knowledge. This is another example of the arrogant Eurocentrism that assumes that unless whites originated the idea it is unworthy of serious consideration. Have we ever called an idea that emerged out of the mind of a white thinker separatist simply because it came from a white person? The black students who study in the classrooms of some of these teachers and professors know more about the term "Afrocentricity" than their professors because they have read the books. The idea that an African American child learns from a stronger position if she is centered, that is, sees herself *in* the story rather than from the margins is not novel (Asante, 2003) but it is revolutionary when we begin to teach teachers how to put the child in the story.

THE CONDITIONS OF EDUCATION

Institutions in a society reflect the character of the society. Crime, education, politics are different in different nations because of the societies. In the United States we have practiced a whites-only-orientation in education. This has had a profound impact on the quality of education for all children. The African American child has suffered out of proportion to white children, who also are victims of diseased curricula. One value of Afrocentric education is that it teaches discipline, that is, it empowers the teacher because discipline is based on the quality of ethical authority that comes from truth. Children submit to discipline to show devotion to a group for which they have respect.

THE TRANSFORMATION OF PERSPECTIVE

Afrocentric education represents a new interpretation of productive transmission of values and attitudes. Students are made to see with new eyes and to hear with new ears. African American children learn to interpret phenomena from themselves as centered; whites learn to see that their own centers are not threatened by the space taken by African Americans or others. Using the strong legs of Afrocentricity a revolutionary pedagogist can reshape the thinking of children about learning. It some senses what the revolutionary pedagogist does is what the African American teachers did during the gloomiest period of segregation; they subverted the system and where they were given the second hand books to bring to the black children sitting in the classroom those teachers, without ever naming themselves, became agents of transformation and made thousands of young black children feel that they could do anything because despite what the texts said or did not say, Africans had built the pyramids and the stone cities of Zimbabwe.

Revolutionary pedagogy works for all children because it is correct and accurate. Now here is the thing: The vast majority of white Americans are ignorant about African American history or culture, yet African Americans study and debate white history and culture. Our black students have vast experiences with the white world and the white world, at least in America, knows next to nothing about black people. Very few white professors have ever had a course in African American Studies and therefore are unable to provide systematic information about African Americans. Unfortunately, much the same is true of black professors who have usually been taught by white professors

We are victims of the same system. Our children do not know the names of the African ethnic groups who comprise our population; we do not know any names of sacred sites in Africa; we can hardly tell you what the Middle Passage was and meant to Africans; and we have forgotten the brutality of slavery and celebration of freedom

THE TRAGEDY OF IGNORANCE OF OUR OWN HISTORY

Our children have little understanding of the nature of the private and state capture, the transport, and enslavement of Africans. How many of us were truly taught the horrors of being taken, shipped naked across twenty five days of ocean, seeing others leap singing to their deaths, being broken by abuse, indignities of all kind, and then dehumanized to a thing without a name? If we knew, perhaps our behavior would be different. If our children had to read the slave narratives, the ship captain's words, they would be different, the white children would be different; America would be a different nation.

They should have heard the story of how the barbaric treatment begin, of how the African's dignity was stolen, and how culture was destroyed. They should know the story of how death swam next to the ships in the dreaded Middle Passage. A few Africans recorded their experiences: Jacob and Ruth Weldon, an African couple, give the most detailed account ever found:(Feldstein, 1971:33-37).

They wrote that the African, having been captured and brought onto the ships, "was chained on the deck, made to bend over, and branded with a red hot iron in the form of letters or signs dipped in an oily preparation and pressed against the naked flesh till it burnt a deep and ineffaceable scar, to show who was the owner" (Feldstein, 1971:p 35).

The Weldons say that "those who screamed were lashed in the face, breast, thighs, and backs with cat-o-nine tails wielded by white sailors. Every blow brought the returning lash pieces of grieving flesh (Feldstein, 1971:pp. 33-37). The Weldons continue that they saw "mothers with babies at their breasts basely branded and lashed, hewed and scarred, till it would seem as if the very heavens must smite the infernal tormentors with the doom they so richly merited" (Feldstein, 1971:36).

If the children of America could read the words of the Weldons who said: "...the male slaves were chained two by two, at the arm and leg. Women were stowed away without chains but naked, and all were packed away in the holes of ships for the five to eight week trip across the sea. The Africans could not even sit upright, the space between the decks being only two feet in height. On fair weather days the Africans were allowed to come on deck and dance for exercise. This they did with leg irons and chains to prevent them from escaping. Even some of the slave ship captains said the "groans and suffocating cries for air and water coming from below the deck sickened the soul of humanity" (Feldstein, 1971:36.)

Compelled to wiggle for space and to moan the long hours of night away in horror, with no fresh water to quench the torment-ing thirst in a tightly squeezed space on the ship, with just enough oxygen to prolong their claustrophobic suffering, our ances-tors vowed in those dark, damp, dank hell holes of horror that we would be free one day. Our children do not know the story. And white children do not know the story. If they were taught the revolutionary pedagogy perspective on the Great Enslavement, they would be different. Remembrance is necessary for humility and understanding. This is why the Jewish community has rightly campaigned to get the European Holocaust taught in schools and colleges across the world. Such a monstrous human brutality should remind the world of how humans have often violated each other. Teaching about the African Holocaust is just as important for some of the same reasons; essentially it underscores the enor-mity of the dislocation of Africans, physically, psychologically, and economically. Without understanding the historical experi-ences of Africans one cannot truly make any headway on dealing with the problems of the present.

There are those who will say that education should begin with the arrival of Africans in the English colonies because that is where African American history begins. That would be a mistake for several reasons. In the first place, 1619 was not the first time that Africans were in the Americas. Furthermore, on the slave ships it is true that the weak perished and that the strong stayed alive, meaning essentially that America became something of a home for those who survived. Yet the experience on the ships created an entirely different history for Africans than for whites who came on their own and most often not against their wills. The Africans' sleeping and resting places were often covered with blood and mucous and the horrid stench of the dead, breeding yet others for death, was everywhere. Those who survived often looked upon the dead beside them and intoned "Gone to she own country" or "gone to he own friends."

INSTRUCTIONAL TESTIMONIES

The slave captains did not spare infants and children from terror. The Weldons tell of a child of nine months being flogged because it would not eat. This failing, the captain ordered the child's feet placed in boiling water which dissolved the skin and nails, then the child was whipped again. Refusing to eat, the child had a piece of mango wood tied to his neck as punishment. When nothing would make this baby eat the captain took him and slammed him from his arms onto the deck. The child died instantly. The mother was called and asked to throw the dead body over board. She refused and was beaten. Then she was forced to take the corpse of her baby to the ship's side, where "with her head averted so she might not see it, she dropped the body into the sea" (Feldstein, 1971:37).

If our children knew the African American's struggle as they ought to know they would find a renewed sense of purpose and vision. If white children knew this, rather than the pablum of deceit which is normally given to them about the European Slave Trade, they would rise up, and not only see differently but work to create a better place. If our children knew that one captain of a ship with 440 Africans on board, had 132 thrown overboard in order to save water! They would cease acting as if they have no past or no reason to live.

When those slave ships reached land, whatever the land, whatever the condition, nothing, the Africans thought, could be as bad as the Middle Passage, with it long bloody night of violence and terror. Here, on land, the situation was often worse. Mothers were often forced to leave their children alone in the slave shacks while they worked in the fields. Unable to nurse these children or to care for them, they often returned from work at night to find their own children dead. (Feldstein, 1971: 49)

If they could really read history and see the relationship of Africans to cotton, women and children working till "the blood runs from the tips of their fingers, where they have been pricked by the hard pod; or if they could see them dragging their baskets, all trembling, to the scale, for fear their weight should be short, and they should get the flogging which in such a case they know they must expect; or if they could see them bent double with constant stooping, and scourged on their bare back when they attempted to rise to straighten themselves for a moment...." (Feldstein, 1971: 49) they would treat each cotton shirt or dress as a sacred fabric just as our brothers and sisters in the Caribbean or in Colombia and Brazil treat sugar with reverence because of the pain it caused our African people.

If they had ever heard the testimony of Henry Bibb who said: "I was born May 1815, of a slave mother...and was claimed as the property of David White, Esq... I was flogged up; for where I should have received moral, mental, and religious instructions,

I received stripes without number, the object of which was to degrade and keep me in subordination. I can truly say, that I drank deeply of the bitter cup of suffering and woe. I have been dragged down to the lowest depths of human degradation and wretchedness, by slaveholders."

CORRECTING DISTORTED INFORMATION

Hegemonic education can only exist so long as true and accurate information is kept from people. With information people have new inputs into reasons, whether they want to follow these paths or not. You can no longer be comfortable with teaching that Greece is the origin of philosophy if you realize that the Greeks taught that Africa, specifically Kemet, was the home of the origin of philosophy. You cannot teach the European origin of art if you know about the black people of ancient Kemet. Hegemonic education can exist only so long as whites think that Africans have never contributed to civilization. It is largely upon such false ideas that invidious distinctions are made.

AFRICAN PHILOSOPHERS

Not only did Africa contribute to human history; African civilizations predate any that we know about since humans originated on the continent of Africa. This is true whether you take archaeological evidence or biological evidence. Let us leave Greece and the Greeks and return to study the Egyptians and Egypt. Let us study the first philosophers: Kagemni, Khun-anup, Ptahhotep, Kete, Duauf, Akhenatonn, Amenomope, Amenemhat, and Seti. But since our education about ourselves is so disjointed we have no way of seeing an organic relationship of Africa to the rest of human history. With our enslavement came an attack on our psychical and spiritual being. The ontological onslaught caused some Africans to opt for suicide; enslavement was a living death, the brutality of the slavocracy is unequalled for its psychological destruction of African Americans. This gave us a freedom faith. However, the results was often *dislocation, disorientation,* and *misorientation;* all conditions of being de-centered. The African in this situation is one who has "shed" or tried to shed race, to become raceless. One's basic identity is self identity which is ultimately cultural identity. Without cultural identity, you are lost. You can no more divest yourself of your race or your culture, than you can stop breathing oxygen and still live. We are African and human; others are European and human, there is no contradiction in either position. Humans come in many types, colors, and cultures. So we have to sing with our ancestors, "Wade in the Waters, children, don't you get weary."

We have been mesmerized, tranquilized, and paralyzed when it comes to education of African American children. Generations before us who came out of the enslavement and became the fastest group of illiterates to ever achieve literacy and who built schools in their churches and taught their families to read and write when only one or two of the family members had any knowledge of English inspire us to construct an authentic response to schools. But we must face up to the challenges that confront pupils each day and defy the negative predictions about the impossible. We know that our history is full of victories over those who have underestimated our ability to succeed. How is it that our ancestors built colleges with pennies and dared to call them universities and some teachers and administrators want to say that African American children cannot be motivated?

Symbols of Resistance

There is the idea that there are two discourses about multiculturalism. Different adherents to the theory have different views on what it means. There is only one discourse that is relevant to the liberation of the minds of African and white people in the United States and that one is based upon the acceptance of Africa as central to African people in terms of *place, location, foundation, history*, as the starting point for any discussion. Diane Ravitch argues that there is a *pluralist multiculturalism* and a **particularist multiculturalism**. I have said this is nonsense because it confuses the fundamental problem we confront in a racist society. These ideas exist only in Ravitch's imagination. Either you are for multiculturalism or you are not. The divisions she advances are really to conceal her position. We can say either a person supports the maintenance of white supremacist teachings and constructions in education or one does not; there is no other possibility. Support of these positions depends upon keeping other people ignorant. Information must be distorted, suppressed, books never written or if written, never published, and if published, banned from the school district. All of the tactics are the tactics of those who prefer Africans on the mental and psychological plantation. Diane Ravitch was called the leader of the professors who opposed multiculturalism in the 1990s. But since their positions are indefensible on that score they argue that they are for multiculturalism which means when you read their works that they are for *a white perspective on everybody else's culture*. I call these professors resisters because they are attempting to resist the progressive transformation of a mono-ethnic curriculum. The resisters say that Afrocentricity is anti-white. If Afrocentricity as a theory is against anything it is against racism, ignorance, and white hegemony in the curriculum. This is not anti-white; it is pro-human. Others have written that it brings about the *tribalization* of America but America already has red state and blue state divisions with a large clan of whites who voted for Donald Trump for example because they saw in him a leader of a tribe that felt threatened and under severe stress because of the increasing multicultural nature of the society. I believe that revolutionary pedagogy provides all Americans an opportunity to accept and promote a more equitable understanding of nation. The reason this is important is because the transmission of common values should be at the center of education. This can only happen if we see that the African person, since the beginning of the nation, has moved from the periphery of the narrative to a place where we all share in the center. No one raises an eyebrow at Chinatowns in America and no one should; yet when African people seek to create from their historical and cultural center they are often met with negative reaction. Is this reaction really about who should be permitted to be on or off of the plantation?

Pluralism is recognition of our difference. America is already divided if you speak of opportunities afforded in education to children. The white child by virtue of the protection provided by the society and enforced by the curriculum is already ahead of the African American child in the first grade. We have got to concentrate on giving the African American child opportunity at the pre-kindergarten level. But the kind of assistance the child needs is as much cultural as academic and must be in tandem with giving the white child the kind of support necessary to diminish the idea of privilege. Indeed, if the cultural information is provided, the academic transformation will follow. The aim of the Afrocentric curriculum and revolutionary pedagogy is not to divide America, but it is to make America flourish, as it ought to flourish.

Some resisters claim that history is being created simply because they do not know the facts. No one has ever proved that history was being created. Can you imagine how arrogant it is for someone to speak of "fantasy history" and "bizarre theories" simply because they have never read the facts or heard the arguments? What they have pointed to is the fact that they did not know something. But it is very arrogant to claim something is created just because you have never heard of it. The only reigning initiative for total change proposed and led by Africans is the movement to transform the curriculum and introduce a new revolutionary pedagogy. Instead of getting on board to fight against white hegemonic education, some whites and some blacks too have decided to plead for a return to the education plantation. However, those days are gone and can never be packaged as accurate, correct education again.

MYTHS ABOUT EDUCATION

We know that our children have been maligned. Our history has been maligned. Our continent of origin has been maligned. We also know that our teachers have often been maligned. But let me give you two truisms about education in America. First, *some teachers can and do effectively teach African American children.* Secondly, *if they can do it, then we can learn what their attitudes are about teaching that makes them successful.* Among the myths we often hear about schools and education are the following:

African American Children have the same advantages as whites. In what school district does this happen?

America has become a nation of criminals, discriminators,

educators who kill little children's motivation. At no point in American history has it been the case that African American children have had the same advantages as whites. You would have to close your eyes to reality in order to make a statement supporting the equality of opportunity. There is not a predominantly African American school in any community in America that is considered the equivalent of the predominantly white school in the same district. I am not talking about brightness of students; I am talking about treatment of the students and expenditures on the schools. The experiences of the Africans are not the same. No other group of people has had such a long campaign against its history and culture. The aim has been to wipe out African identity. There are several myths that add to the misinformation about education. Those who provide information are often operating on the basis of these false myths.

Treatment of African American Children is the same as for whites: In which school is this really the case?

If you believe this myth, then you are ready to be sold the George Washington Bridge. Whether you speak of the historical relationship to school environment, textbook publishers, boards of education, or teacher responses to the children; our children are not treated equally. I am not saying, treated the same, I am saying treated equally.

Most of all, context for learning is different, names of buildings, models for learning experiences, trips to places of cultural value to the students, and invitation to writers and speakers.

There is ample information about Africans in the Curriculum. Why would someone make such an ignorant statement when the entire curriculum is about white people and their deeds and misdeeds?

School curricula see Africans as guests; consequently there is little modeling of events and personalities. White students may ask the teacher who teaches about Africans, Is it going to be on the test? If not, then they often do not consider the information as an organic part of the subject under discussion. Why should a little African child have to see herself as a guest when her ancestors are interwoven with the building of the nation?

STRATEGIES FOR IMPLEMENTATION

There are several steps necessary for implementing a revolutionary pedagogy and an Afrocentric curriculum for change. Indeed, the attention to language in the scope and sequence of the curriculum is one of the easiest ways to assess the situation in a school curriculum. What type of words and terms are used to refer to African peoples? Are these words pejoratives? Can they be changed to reflect the realities of the situation. Among the steps to be considered are the following points for discussion:

1. Language issues: Pay attention to terms such as *Slavery, Bushman, Pygmies, minority, co-culture, sub cultures, Black Africa, tribe,* and phrases like "a bunch of wild Indians," etc.
2. Strong involvement of teachers, parents; churches need after school schools
3. Understand the ideas of *scope, sequence*, and *objectives* as they relate to curriculum
4. De-bias attitudes as well as facts by looking for assertions that are biased in the way they are stated.

RADICAL INTRODUCTION OF AFRICAN CONTENT

Afrocentric education is a radical introduction of African content into the curriculum in an effort to change the quality of the educational experience for African American students and to create enough factual bases for a new understanding of knowledge by other students. However, it is not mere contributionism that is the center of Afrocentric education; but integrated and infused information. Afrocentric education is therefore a fundamental necessity for anyone declaring competence in almost any subject in America; otherwise the person remains essentially ignorant of a major portion of the world. Thus, Afrocentric infusion is a core element in revolutionary pedagogy.

Furthermore, multiculturalism, to be authentic, must consider the Afrocentric perspective that is the proper stepping-stone from the African American culture to a true multiculturalism. If this step is skipped we are likely to see an idea of multiculturalism as defined through the eyes of whites without any substantive African American information infused in the curriculum. I think that we are fairly clear that as we march toward revolutionary pedagogy we can neither skip Afrocentric curriculum nor proper multiculturalism. They are incorporated into the new orientation to education.

CHAPTER FOUR

The Principles of the Pedagogy of Revolution

I arrive at revolutionary pedagogy from my position as a descendant of enslaved Africans knowing full well that all education originates from intentions, obligations, desires, and ambitions one finds in societies. To change the nature of pedagogy and the content of curriculum mean that we must also change the nature of the society's objectives for educating the people. This is the revolution that must happen to insure the effective and useful education of children.

This book deals with the politics of education and analyzes how we must overturn the oppressive conditions of education and create a revolutionary pedagogy. My objective is to make it possible for the teacher to challenge all forms of racist knowledge and to assert through a powerful pedagogical ethic a new vision of education.

I do not think that teachers generally express racist views. I do not believe that administrators of schools think that they are supporting racism. Yet in most instances they are doing nothing to challenge the oppressive symbols, images, ideas, concepts, content or pedagogy that exist in their schools. The truth of the matter is that without a conscious reading and thinking about teaching you will undoubtedly create or recreate racial pedagogy.

REVOLUTIONARY PEDAGOGY AND NECESSARY OBJECTIVES

Here is what a revolutionary pedagogy must do:

- It must challenge the educational vision perpetrated by the oppressive system of racism;
- It must defend students from the self-hatred that invades their spirits;
- It must play a role in supporting agency for those who have been marginalized by the system of education in terms of concepts, themes, and curricular ideas.

It must demonstrate methods for combatting agency reduction in the academy; and it must counteract and contradict negations of African agency and narratives.

Any idea that education is neutral is nothing more than political posturing. All education is political and has lifestyle and policy implications. In a revolutionary pedagogy we seek to expose all myths of educational neutrality promoted by those who control the reins of power. In effect, a revolutionary pedagogy is subversive to the oppressive curriculum that is meant to mold the minds of children to be consumers, clients, and victims. In this respect revolutionary pedagogy opposes the sexist and racist indoctrination that is often a serious component of the curricula of American education. I do not mean that this occurs in an overt manner because most of the time it is a covert racism and sexism, something that is not expressed but practiced, and lived.

One of the challenges of revolutionary pedagogy is to charge the status quo with hiding behind the idea of universalism. Whether this is the assertion that science has a universal character or that what is considered classical is universal the idea is false and consequently at the core of what must be overturned. Those who say, "Get politics out of schools," are the very ones who are maintaining politics in schools. It is disconcerting that those who attack racism and sexism in the curriculum are considered subversive while those who use the curriculum to represent the status quo are considered mainstream.

How revolutionary pedagogy can be applied to change the focus of education so that students benefit is the subject of this project. We all know that racism or racial hegemony is not merely a physical issue, but an issue of ideas, art, and practice. Thus, the abstract becomes real, the symbolic is presented in the act of teaching, and pedagogy comes alive because of the teacher.

Carter G. Woodson, Mary McLeod Bethune, Asa Hilliard, Barbara Sizemore, Jawanza Kunjufu, and Joyce King have been some of the boldest champions of transformative education in the history of America. In Woodson's case he wrote in the *Miseducation of the Negro* that the African American was not properly educated because he was educated away from himself, from history, from his own narratives. Woodson once wrote, "If you can control a man's thinking you do not have to worry about his action. When you determine what a man shall think you do not have to concern yourself about what he will do. If you make a man feel that he is inferior, you do not have to compel him to accept an inferior status, for he will seek it himself. If you make a man think that he is justly an outcast, you do not have to order him to the back door. He will go without being told; and if there is no back door, his very nature will demand one." Woodson was a revolutionary in the sense that he wanted African Americans to study their own history and culture as a base for following other forms and avenues of education. He was well aware that it was not in the interest of white to properly educate blacks; this had to be something that blacks would take up. Thus, "Philosophers have long conceded, however, that every man has two educators: 'that which is given to him, and the other that which he gives himself. Of the two kinds the latter is by far the more desirable. Indeed all that is most worthy in man he must work out and conquer for himself. It is that which constitutes our real and best nourishment. What we are merely taught seldom nourishes the mind like that which we teach ourselves" (Woodson, 2013).

In my judgment it is impossible to move children to the point of wanting to study or acquire knowledge if they do not have a truly radical reading of history. All scholars who have studied the nature of information have concluded that oppressors will never teach the oppressed how to break their chains; this they must do for each other. It was Woodson who anticipated revolutionary pedagogy and I have always paid respect to him the chapter on the Afrocentric Idea in Education. I was further encouraged by Woodson's strong belief that we had learned the music and culture of everyone but Africans. So Woodson said, "...to handicap a student by teaching him that his black face is a curse and that his struggle to change his condition is hopeless is the worst sort of lynching" (Woodson, 2013) I think today he would add to teach children by commission or omission that their ancestors never created civilizations, culture, inventive tool or arts is also a form of lynching, mental lynching.

Mary McLeod Bethune called for Africans to assert heroes and monuments and personalities to demonstrate the strength and brilliance of African people. In her famous speech "Clarifying our Vision with the Facts" delivered on October 31, 1937 before the Association for the Study of Negro Life and History, Bethune said of black children "When they learn of the fairy tales of mythical king and queen and princess, we must let them hear, too, of the pharaohs and African kings and brilliant pageantry of the Nile Valley; when they learn of Caesar and his legions we must teach them of Hannibal and his Africans; when they learn of Shakespeare and Goethe we must teach them of Pushkin and Dumas." So powerful was Bethune's remembrances of the glorious history of African people, founded on the same philosophy that she had used to bring into existence her organization National Council of Negro Women two years earlier in 1935, that high leaders of the nation, including the First Lady Eleanor Roosevelt were influenced by her. In many ways Bethune and Woodson were on the same wavelength. Woodson said, "If you teach the Negro that he has accomplished as much good as any other race he will aspire to equality and justice without regard to race. Such an effort would upset the program of the oppressor in Africa and America. Play up before the Negro, then, his crimes and shortcomings. Let him learn to admire the Hebrew, the Greek, the Latin and the Teuton. Lead

the Negro to detest the man of African blood—to hate himself."
Bethune and Woodson knew, as other educatorwas the educator
who offered love of the children as a central revolutionary idea.
Furthermore as a master teacher himself and a brilliant trainer of
teachers he would often say, "I have never encountered any children in any group who were not geniuses. There is no mystery on
how to teach them. The first thing you do is to treat them like
human beings and the second thing is to love them." And he knew
that when you begin to do things that will raise the achievement
levels of the poorest and disenfranchised students "you may not
get applause." Hilliard also argued that there were two reasons for
knowing African heritage in education, child-raising, or socialization. He says "we have the best teaching and socialization practices ever developed and the primary tool of our oppression is
mis-education (www.kintespace.com/kp_asa0.html). Hilliard's
main contention was that teaching had to be seen as a sacred work
because the teacher had to tap into the spiritual realm in order
to focus on making the community better through the positive
teaching of children. The African teacher cannot see the children
as clients or customers; they must see them as the continuation of
a divine work (www.kintespace.com/kp_asa0.html).

In several of his speeches Asa Hilliard declared that the proper
orientation for teachers had to be, among other things, the beliefs
that the cosmos is alive, that spirituality is the center of our being,
that African people have a divine purpose and destiny, that each
child is a Living Sun, that children can move toward perfection
to be more like the creator, that Maat should be the focus of the
curriculum, that knowledge of self is the premium knowledge,
that mastery is possible and desirable, the genius and divinity

of children are reflected in intellect, humanity, and spirit, and that teaching is itself a calling toward mastery (Hilliard, 1998). Hilliard had arrived at these conclusions after a long career as Dean of Education at San Francisco State University and distinguished professor at Georgia State University.

Barbara Sizemore gave her life for the revolutionary pedagogy where children were taught to learn and not to be forced to learn at a certain speed. "It is not so much how fast a child reads but whether or not a child reads at any rate," Sizemore said.

Jawanza Kunjufu argued that black boys were under threat almost from the time they entered school and there needed to be a stronger attempt to rescue boys from the damages of the education system.

Joyce King writes about narratives of memory and shows us how an Afrocentric pedagogy can lean toward revolution. She knows that education is what is being done now. There is no education but that which is being practiced.

While it is easy to say that the scientific revolution brought into being the separation of value and fact, matter and spirit, it is not so easy to see how the European Enlightenment and the scientific revolution ever dealt with racist myths. One might even say that the European Enlightenment was the height of European notions of superiority and hence was among the most backward moments in European history despite the propaganda to the contrary.

The goals of a revolutionary pedagogy are clear:

In revolutionary pedagogy we seek to make children appreciate their own histories and cultures as integrated into all system of knowing. That is, children must not feel when they leave your class that they are outside of the subject you are teaching. The revolutionary teacher pulls the child into the circle of the subject.

The revolutionary pedagogist demands that students are aware of other ethnic and cultural groups and their contributions to human knowledge. I deliberately use the term "pedagogist" in a new way so as to unhinge it from the Greek ideas of a young male slave supervising the children of a master which is usually rendered as "pedagogue." The pedagogist is a conscious interpreter of signs and symbols that constitute the educational architecture of a society. In fact, a pedagogist is not merely a supervisor, but an active participant in the construction of a revolutionary knowledge. This means that the pedagogist must search out the information that will allow him or her to wield this incredible power in the classroom.

Revolutionary pedagogy obliterates cultural ignorance at every turn by employing the techniques of transmitting knowledge based on facts with an eye toward community values of truth, order, balance, harmony, justice, and reciprocity.

A revolutionary pedagogy therefore is a projection of the will to be human among other humans and to protect the legacies of humanity. Nothing is easy about this but it is achievable when teachers are good people transmitting information. The revolutionary teacher is just such a person, gifted with knowledge of a particular subject, filled with inexhaustible passion for teaching, and willing to demonstrate techniques that bring all students into the arena of human achievement.

In the American context one thing has been clear as long as the society has had educational institutions and that is that those institutions were never designed primarily as sites for black education. In other words, black people were never seen as the source and origin of the process. No school system, for example, was designed with blacks students as the primary subjects. That is precisely why we have had so many "correctives" intended to adjust the education system, the curriculum, and the pedagogy for black children, and indeed, for all other than white children. This is a problem for all teachers and students and it remains one of the overwhelming issues to be confronted by revolutionary pedagoy. The oppressive nature of schooling as Mwalimu Shujaa mentioned in his book, *Too Much Schooling, Too Little Education: The Paradox of Black Live in White Societies*, "Education is our means of providing fo reht the inter-generational transmission of values, beliefs, traditions, customs, rituals and sensibilities along with the knowledge of why these things must be sustained" (Shujaa, Africa World Press, 1994, Introduction). Shujaa is essentially criticizing the way black children have been educated in the American society.

A horrendous record of mis-education of black children confronts every school district in the United States. Our children are suffering under a reign of intellectual terrorism where most teachers cannot identify five African ethnic groups brought to the Americas during the enslavement era. So problematic is this terrorism that we are forced to witness the slow destruction of the students' brains as information about the diaspora is woefully lacking in schools. If you were to ask students in high school to name the country in the Americas with the largest populations of Africans few would be able to give a good guess so tragic is the lack of information about the European Slave Trade in our public schools.

I think that the only way to achieve any sense of revolutionary direction in pedagogy is to re-orient toward a new emphasis on proper content. For example, if a teacher is going to teach about Africa she should teach all of Africa and dispense with the old broken formula of Africa South of the Sahara or Sub-Saharan terms. The Sahara is a desert on the continent of Africa just as the Mojave is a desert in the country of the United States. Breaking the back of the orthodoxy will require a commitment to new regime of knowledge.

Consequently, revolutionary pedagogy must no longer teach children about a geographical area called the Middle East. This is not just bad geography; it is politics and has no fundamental relationship to the truth about anything in Africa. There is no Middle Eastern part of Africa. Indeed the idea of the Middle East is a 20th century phenomenon established in the literature after the founding of the state of Israel. In one swell swoop, so to speak, writers could speak of Israel and its Arab neighbors as living in the Middle East. Technically this term does not stand a chance of survival in revolutionary pedagogy because to be in the "middle east" actually depends upon where you start your visualization. In fact, to the Chinese, Germany might be the Middle East. It is said that the sun rises in the east and sets in the west but the east and the west is always changing as the sun races across the sky. Revolutionary pedagogists will abandon the idea of the middle-east because it is a testament to Eurocentric conceptualizations of space.

As far as we know now human beings as homo sapiens originated in East Africa, somewhere between Ethiopia and Tanzania. And since that time homo sapiens have been balancing commonalities and diversities with unending periods of great tension, stress, and warfare, seeking to right the perceived slights and wrongs of other humans. There has rarely been a period of time on the earth that humans have been completely free of conflict. Although conflicts might not exist in one area of the world, they are sure to exist in another during the same period as the season of peace in the first area.

PRACTICE BREAKING BARRIERS

Most children in the United States have a negative view of Africa. Africans do not base such a perception of Africa on anything the students have read in books; these perceptions are most likely the results of media sources and general historic ignorance about the continent. How to break the myths as we would break a toothpick is the question? A teacher can simply introduce new information and evidence that contradicts the old myth. This is probably the most direct way to challenge false ideas.

Once again the revolutionary pedagogist seeks to unravel all forms of twisted thinking about Africa in order to prepare the groundwork for inspiring performance, attracting interest, and attaching students to content. I once sat in a classroom in a large metropolitan city in the Midwest as the teacher told the students about lions and tigers in the African jungle. I wanted to go through the floor because I just knew that at any moment a student would jump up and say, "Ms. Caroline, there are no tigers in Africa." No student caught the mis-statement and Ms. Caroline did not seem to realize that tigers were Asian animals. Later I told her that information and then informed her that jungle is not a good identification of the topography of Africa. The continent is mostly grassland and rainforest and neither classifies as jungle.

Clearly the notion that Africa is dangerous circulates between teachers, schools, universities, and other institutions. It is a very difficult myth that must be broken. There are so many young people from Europe, the Americas and Asian now traveling around the continent with no major concerns about safety because unless you happen upon a war there is no place in Africa that you have to fear the local population. The general African idea to human beings is that they are human until they prove that they are *unhuman*.

I find that most people who live in Africa do not find it dangerous, too hot, or too damp for human beings. It is a much-loved continent so much so that whites that have settled in Kenya, South Africa, Ivory Coast or Namibia do not want to leave. Some areas of Africa are deeply urban and have long histories of urbanization; hence cities such as Lagos, now called the most populated city in the world with 28 million people, or Cape Town, Durban, Johannesburg, Nairobi, Abidjan, Dakar, or Addis Ababa are as sophisticated as any cities you will find on any other continent. To some degree this is function of global capital that cannot be underestimated in producing similar technologies around the world, but on the other hand, Africans have approached the new situation with African sentiments, aesthetics, and sensibilities.

The history of Africa is long; the history of humans in Africa is the longest in the world. So it is interesting that there are still people insisting that Africa has no history. This Hegelian notion has refused to die although it has been assaulted for the past sixty years by some of the best African minds. Cheikh Anta Diop, Theophile Obenga, Teshale Tibebu, and others have demonstrated that Hegel's original 1828 idea about Africa having no history was maliciously wrong. What is history anyway? Who gets to tell the narrative and who gets to record it? How is it propagated and who subscribes to it? These are all questions about power and the revolutionary pedagogist must bring these issues up on the classroom.

I once thought that the classroom should be free of difficult ideas but if one is not able to discuss difficult ideas in the classroom, and really, think about it, these are not difficult ideas, then where are we to discuss them. Why do you think we have such illiteracy among adults who can read! Literacy cannot be just about knowing your ABCs; it must be about knowing how to change your life because you understand concepts and ideas.

Critical thinking is now a base rock for educational thinking yet it is hardly about the kind of critical thinking that will help African American children. Raise questions that are pointed to their history and culture. In the 1990s a teacher at a small school near Philadelphia was telling his class that the only people who ever domesticated elephants were Indians from Asia when a young girl, about 14 stood up and asked him, "Is it true that Hannibal's army trained elephants to cross the alps?" The teacher did not know how to answer the student and rather than saying, "Let me look into that," simply repeated that only Indian elephants were trainable. Doubling down never means that you are right; it is like an ostrich digging its head deeper into the ground. The answer to the question is "Yes, Hannibal the Great, of African Khart Haddas, often called Carthage, led his elephants over the alps to fight with the Romans."

Another myth is that all Africans are the same. When people say this or think this it is important to know what they mean. There are nearly 3000 languages spoken on the continent of Africa making it the most diverse continent on earth. To say that all Africans are the same is not to take into consideration the immense diversity of histories, heroics, travel, adventure, politics, art, culture, and religion on the continent. Even with this diversity, however, there are certain common traits found among African ethnic groups. Usually scholars say that most Africans have a special place for ancestor reverence in their philosophical systems. This means that whether one is from Ghana in West Africa or South Africa or Kenya there are certain values that tend to be similar. So one has to say that common values exist but different histories also exist. The Zulu and the Asante people are not the same in specific histories but they both share a common approach to ancestors.

Here are ten common values found throughout Africa.

1. Respect and Reverence For The Ancestors
2. Character Is The Greatest Virtue For Relationship
3. Fertility In The Sense of Reproduction Is A High Value
4. Collective and Communal Values Are Consistent With African Societies
5. Discovering One's Destiny And Living It is Important
6. Agrarian Values Dominate Most Societies
7. Evolving toward Community Harmony
8. Late Weaning Of Children
9. Music And Dance Are Of The Same Fabric
10. Respect For Elders

Using these value in lesson plans or as foundations for discussing academic subjects and themes in classrooms is a way to support revolutionary pedagogy. What is intended by listing these values is that the teacher will have solid African cultural values to explore in building classroom discourse. Take the idea of respect for elders among many African communities and you will see that this idea can be evaluated and utilized in social studies classes. Revolutionary pedagogists will sometimes ask that students bring their grandparents or grand-aunts and uncles to the school classroom to engage in cultural remembering conversations. Stories that elders have to tell are often quite striking and motivating to students. So in revolutionary pedagogy it is often said, "Let the elders speak!" Consequently, encouragement of elders to visit the classrooms and recount their experiences is a way to build community solidarity and to impart values by demonstrations.

CHAPTER FIVE

Essential Knowledge for Revolutionary Teachers

Teachers Do The Best They Can

Teachers teach what they know. It is to be expected that teachers will not be able to teach what they do not know. In fact, some teachers actually do not want to know what it is that they do not know. Yet to be an effective teacher there are some assumptions a teacher of African American, Native American, Latino, and Asian children need to embrace. I do not mention European descended students only because they are the default group in American education.

One of the key aspects of teaching is knowing who it is that you are teaching. If you do not know the children sitting in the classroom you will not be consistently successful as a teacher. Who are these children? Are they in good fettle? What do they eat for breakfast or do they eat at all? What kinds of families they come from or are they living with guardians? What kind of music do they listen to and what excites them about popular culture? What are they expected to know about your topic?

Answering as many of these questions as you can prior to teaching a class will help tremendously. In fact, at some level the teacher might be able to catch up to this information by asking some of the less embarrassing questions on the first day of class. The revolutionary pedagogist never forgets that the main goal is to get the student to learn. A teacher is not a teacher until the pupil has learned. This is why analyzing the classroom affords the teacher an advantage over those teachers who assume they know what they are talking about and do not need any analysis.

First, a teacher must assume that he or she does not know everything they need to know to be able to teach the children in their classrooms. This does not mean that you do not know your subject, one for which you have paid dearly in time and struggle as well as money to acquire, it simply means that there are cultural and historical artifacts that you do not know. Learning is pragmatic and demonstrative for the students; the teacher must model that behavior and not show closed eyes or mind.

Secondly, a teacher must realize that students attend to what they are interested in and this is the best approach to attaching them to the subject. Gaining the attention of students and having them participate in learning is a technique that must be studied and practiced with patience and humility. Attracting students to a topic or theme depends upon a combination of pedagogical skills that are attainable through knowledge. *The principal rule of revolutionary pedagogy is that all classroom behaviors are controlled through superior knowledge*. The teacher who is willing to submit to such knowledge, can and will be very successful in the classroom. I will lay this out more clearly in the following pages.

Thirdly, a teacher, to be revolutionary, must challenge all orthodoxies when the situations in the classroom demand it. This is not challenge for the sake of obstruction, deviance, or comedy, but for seizing moments for knowledge intervention. The best teachers are those teachers who can understand and appreciate how to challenge the canards of practice and create innovation, interest, and color in the classroom. Students appreciate teachers who teach differently just because those teachers are the ones who do not think that there is something wrong with the new generation. They embrace revolution.

WHAT TEACHERS NEED TO UNDERSTAND ABOUT EDUCATION

In revolutionary pedagogy we look for teachers who are able to read and understand the great diversity of our students. I have simplified the process by suggesting that we need to study the ideas of perspective, agency, and location. These are fundamental tools of Afrocentric education and as useful concept in teaching they have the potential of being revolutionary. We generally say that the idea of perspective leans in different directions depending upon your view of the world. Afrocentrists tend to see openness, straightforwardness, trust, and consistency when it comes to evaluating a situation, judging a fact, or responding to an individual. On the other hand it is suggested that through the eyes of whites perspective may conjure up that which is secret, duplicitous, suspicious, and inconsistency.

Moving to agency the Afrocentrist seek collective actualizing, and is motivated by shame, openness, and personal relations as opposed to the more Eurocentric idea of individual actualizing, guilt, secrecy, and impersonal relationships. Each of these represents values that we find in our society. Ultimately we have to proclaim centeredness, trust, and balance as opposed to absolute fluidity, suspicion, and being unsettled.

Given this set of binaries, homologies and antipathies it should not be a surprise to discover that this bifurcation extends to our concept of society as well. African people have met Europe in many spheres and over the past five hundred years have experienced an inordinate amount of the most aggressive human greed and brutality. Most of Europe cannot teach us society, civilization, democracy, law, ethics, human relations or values; its history has been the antithesis of those ideas. Africans gave the world the full meaning of the concept of freedom from oppression. Two hundred and forty six years of enslavement gave a warrant to Africans to make freedom the hallmark of struggle. In every era and at all times African Americans have had to confront agency reduction formations in all sectors of the society. Education is no exception as a locus of confrontation where African Americans are up against curriculum and pedagogy that act to reduce agency.

LEARNING TO RECOGNIZE DYSCONSCIOUS RACISM

Joyce King says that dysconscious racism "denotes the limited and distorted understanding students have about inequity and cultural diversity—-understandings that make it difficult for them to act in favor of truly equitable education" (King, 1991:134). A revolutionary pedagogist must learn to recognize dysconscious racism, that is, the situations where teachers may not have an intention of practicing racism but the results of their behaviors, methods, and temperaments are nevertheless just as if they were based on racial animosity. King sees situations where a teacher might discover that her white students might be threatened emotionally by Afrocentric infusion methods, liberatory curriculum, or revolutionary pedagogy teacher educator. In such cases, King, one of the most progressive educators in America, suggests that the teacher might need to reconstruct social knowledge and self-identity. Of course, the reconstruction may not happen until the teacher realizes that she is agitated by the new information. It would be best if the teacher education program or professional development program could prepare the teacher to confront this possibility in herself or in her students prior to the classroom experience.

As a practical matter I have always felt that the best method of steeling the teacher against dysconscious racism was to teach the teacher how to recognize and deal with oppression. King goes so far as to elevate this idea alongside the reconstruction of self-identity as a technique to deal with dysconscious racism. If you cannot identify oppression then you will not be able to combat it in your classroom. For the revolutionary pedagogist identification and treatment of dysconscious racism are important to the process of bringing into existence authentic revolutionary pedagogy.

If a teacher is unable to identify racism or color privilege then that teacher will have a difficult time in an urban classroom. Some teachers participate in dysconscious racism because they are clueless about racial oppression. I do not believe that these teachers are necessarily racist themselves but they are participants in dysconscious racism. What one hopes is that such teachers would

study various situations in order to gain a more empathetic understanding of how racism in all of its forms has challenged students
culturally, ethically, and politically.

APPRECIATING THE CLASSICAL AFRICAN PHILOSOPHY OF LEARNING

It goes without saying that most educators are familiar with various theories and theorists of education in the Western world. It
is common to hear teachers speak of John Dewey's pragmatism,
Hegelian ideas, and Social Darwinism, as aspects of European intellectual thoughts. Primarily because we have been trained in the
West which is extremely high on itself, we know the Greek influ-
ence on education and have some understanding of how Greece
and Rome, that is Greek and Latin, played major roles in European education. We know next to nothing about how classical Africa created initiations, rituals of excellence, discipline study, and
methods of transmission of information to disciples. To be effective as a revolutionary pedagogist the teacher must appreciate the
origin of African history and knowledge.

Herodotus, Clement of Alexandria, and Diodorus, three
ancient Greeks among others, claim that the ancient Africans of
Egypt had six specific grades of students. The levels of education,
in some way or another, represented the paths of initiates toward
higher and higher information found in other African societies. A
student had to master the knowledge in a particular grade before
he or she could move on; in effect, the Africans laid the foundation
for the class grade levels we now find in most educational systems.
Students had to master certain books of Tehuti often called by
the Greeks, Hermes or Thoth. According to Clement as reported

by George James in *Stolen Legacy*, the description of the order of
priestly education in the *Egyptian Mysteries* went like the following:

> "First comes the singer *Odus*, bearing an instrument of music.
> He has to know by heart two of the books of Tehuti; one
> containing the hymns of the Gods, and the other, the allot-
> ment of the king's life. Next comes the *Horoscopus,* carrying
> in his hand a horologium or sun-dial, and a palm branch; the
> symbols of Astronomy. He has to know four of the books
> of Hermes, which deal with Astronomy. Next comes the
> *Hierogrammat*, with feathers on his head, and a book in his
> hand, and a rectangular case with writing materials, i.e., the
> writing ink and the reed. He has to know the hieroglyphics,
> cosmography, geography, astronomy, the topography of
> Egypt, the sacred utensils and measures, the temple furniture
> and the lands. Next comes the *Stolistes,* carrying the cubit of
> justice, and the libation vessels. He has to know the books
> of Hermes that deal with the slaughter of animals. Next
> comes the *Prophetes* carrying the vessel of water, followed by
> those who carry the loaves. The *Prophetes* has to know the
> ten books that are called hieratic, and contain the laws and
> doctrines concerning the secret theology Gods-theology)
> and the whole education of the Priests. The books of Hermes
> are 42 in number and are absolutely necessary. 36 of them
> have to be known by the Orders that precede and contain
> the whole philosophy of the Egyptians. The remaining six
> books must be known by the Order of *Pastophori*. These are
> medical books and deal with physiology, male and female
> diseases, anatomy, drugs and instruments. The books of
> Hermes were well known to the ancient world and were

known to Clement of Alexandria, who lived at the beginning of the third century A.D." (James, 2014: 96)

SIX LEVELS OF ANCIENT EGYPTIAN EDUCATION

These six levels: *odus, horoscopus, hierogrammat, stolistes, prophetes*, and *pastophori* encompassed a complete curriculum for those who would teach others. In the West the educational system has evolved to the point where a student who would be a teacher simply majors in a field and then take certain practical courses in education to assist with the preparation of course outlines, lesson plans, and alignments to certain standards by the state or institution. Obviously this type of education is not designed in a revolutionary manner; the aim of this structure is to maintain the status quo not to overturn it or to disturb the students' cocoon. Revolutionary pedagogy aims to bring about a transformation in the information, presentation of the information, and transformation of the teacher, hence making the teacher subscribe personally to a revolutionary agenda. I want nothing more than for a student to walk out of your classroom and say, "I have learned something that I had not even thought about but I know I will never be the same after this class!" This is not an uncommon statement even among students who have not been consistently exposed to revolutionary materials, but it can be even more common and less stressful if you think of teaching as a subversive act because you are trying to move students off of the old terms.

BEGINNING THE LESSON WITH THE BEGINNING

I was never very fond of remembering dates when I was an elementary and high school student. Somehow the rote memory of dates seemed pointless to my young mind; it would be many decades before I appreciated the value of dates. Increasingly, over the years I have concluded that the most important aspect of the lesson plan is the starting place and that is what my teachers did not understand. I would have been much farther along in critical thinking had I mastered the understanding of the beginning.

Revolutionary pedagogy demands that a teacher starts with origins and definitions because this is where one sets the stage for a child to learn in context. If you do not have a sense of time it will be hard to establish a location and without a location in the subject field you may end up with distorted information. Consequently, a person could be studying cell theory in biology and not know that among the first scientists to write about cell theory was the African American Ernest Just in the 1940s. Knowing biology is one thing but knowing that Ernest Just was an early pioneer in a specific field of biology allows students, of all backgrounds, to appreciate the primacy of Just's discoveries. Without this understanding a teacher may teach biology without being able to attach the African American child to the subject. I think it is a good exercise for teachers to explore all the possibilities for connections to the students even if it takes a little more time. There is nothing that humans have done a long time that other humans have not been able to do. So giving the origins and giving the definitions of concepts go hand in hand with revolutionary pedagogy.

ASSUMPTIONS OF A REVOLUTIONARY PEDAGOGY

Teachers rarely get the training they need for revolutionary pedagogy; that is why professional development for teachers is essential. Any school district or school that tries to get ahead without some development work with teachers will fail. It is impossible to teach in urban schools districts whether Atlanta or Detroit, San Francisco or San Antonio, without some solid culturally relevant training, preferably revolutionary pedagogy. Here are three foundational blocks of revolutionary pedagogy:

1. Human beings originated on the African continent.
2. All human migration to other parts of the world left from Africa.
3. The originators of geometry, sculpture, medicine, philosophy, and astronomy were Africans.

The reader may be thinking, "Why is it necessary to state these assumptions?" Mainly it is necessary because there are many people who still believe that these assumptions are false contrary to the reports of all scientists. Nevertheless, for revolutionary pedagogy you must know and accept these assumptions because without them everything that comes after will seem confusing and contradictory. We must argue for the right of students to be taught from the standpoint of their own agency. This depends upon knowledge of the origin and migration of humans and other factors in the development and emergence of knowledge.

The Origin and Migration of Humans

As far as scientists know *homo sapiens* originated in East Africa and spread to the rest of the earth. It is fair to say that before 70,000 years ago all humans were black. Leaving Africa, *homo sapiens* made it to the ends of the earth in less than 30,000 years. When civilization takes hold in the Nile River Valley numerous people from Uganda to the Mediterranean Sea added to the narrative of society. Writing, medicine, architecture, domestication of animals, naming of the stars, creation of the calendar, and mathematics became formidable foundations for all knowledge. The educator who is able to lock in this information will be able to appreciate the lesson plans that will attach the students to contemporary subjects.

A Litany of Unsung Names from African History to Be Used in Lesson Plans as Necessary

I have chosen to write the names of some Africans that you may not have heard about, yet they are integral to an understanding and appreciation of African culture and history. Teachers should master several of these names in terms of their historical narrative, their work, and their place in world history.

Menes: The African king who united 42 communities along the Nile River.

Imhotep: African builder of the first pyramid and first physician in history.

Amenhotep, son of Hapu: Ancient African who was considered the person "who knew all there was to know."

Ramses II: One of the greatest African monarch's in history and the builder of many monuments.

Thutmoses III: The African who was the greatest conquering king in history.

Hatshepsut: The most prominent African female leader in the ancient world.

Queen Tiye: The African woman who influenced many leaders of the 18th dynasty.

Taharka: One of the greatest African leaders who united Kemet with Nubia.

Cheikh Anta Diop: Considered the greatest African intellectual of the 20th century.

W. E. B. Du Bois: The author of 33 books and the most distinguished African American intellectual of the 20th century.

Nat Turner: Iconic leader of the 1831 revolt against slavery.

Ahmad Baba: Author of 42 books and the last chancellor of the University of Sankore in Timbuktu.

Cheikh Omar Tall: Born in Futa Toro in the late 18th century he became one of the most important generals fighting against the French.

Kwame Nkrumah: The greatest proponent of Pan Africanism and the first president of Ghana.

Amadou Bamba: The spiritual leader of the Mourrides brotherhood in Senegal.

Sundiata: The most noble name in the gallery of West African empire builders.

Nzingha: The queen who led her armies against the Portuguese in the Congo and Angola region.

Hintsa kaKhawuta: The 13th king of the amaXhosa nation led the most powerful kingdom in the Eastern Cape.

Shaka kaSenzangakhona: The great Zulu king who created a mighty martial nation in the early 19th century in Southern Africa.

Paul Robeson: African American singer who was a Civil Rights spokesperson in the 20th century.

Nanny of the Maroons: A Jamaican national hero, who was a leader of the maroons who fought the English colonialists in the 18th century.

Zumbi: African Brazilian hero associated with the quilombo that claimed independence from the Portuguese colonialists.

Paul Bogle: Jamaican national hero who fought for the legitimate rights of blacks in Jamaica.

Dessalines: Haitian who defeated Napoleon's army in 1804.

Abubakari: Malian king who sent hundreds of ships toward the Americas in 1311-12.

Abdias do Nascimento: The most important African Brazilian intellectual and social rights leader of the 20th century.

Booker T. Washington: Founder of Tuskegee Institute.

Mary McLeod Bethune: Founder of Bethune-Cookman College and the founder of the National Council of Negro Women.

Nelson Mandela: First democratically elected president of South Africa.

Yanga: African who led a revolt against the Spanish in Mexico.

Manuel Zapata Olivella: One of the most important African Colombian writers of the 20th century.

Mansa Musa: The African emperor who has been called "the richest man in the history of the world."

Vicente Guerrero: First Mexican president who was the first African descendant president of a North American country.

Barack Obama: First African American president in the United States.

Kwame Ture: One of the most popular leaders of the Student Nonviolent Coordinating Committee.

Marcus Garvey: Heroic leader of the Universal Negro Improvement Association and African Communities League who organized 10 million blacks.

Langston Hughes: One of the greatest poets of the Harlem Renaissance period.

Nicolas Guillen: African Cuban poet who was the national poet laureate of Cuba.

Menelik II: The powerful Ethiopian emperor who defeated the Italian army at Adwa.

Hannibal Barca: African king who led Khart-Haddas against Rome during the 3rd century BC.

These are just a few of the names that teachers who teach black children should know, just as a matter of course. The comments are truncated and I hope that the revolutionary pedagogist will add to this information or have students research these individuals and others. Understanding and appreciating the use of these names and the histories and dramas that come with them would greatly enrich the teaching experience and bring the students into the context of your topic, whatever it is! You could experiment by classifying these names and others into philosophers, scientists, poets, military leaders, and resistance fighters. Add to the list and have students research others that should be added. This list is merely suggestive.

AFRICAN DESCENDED WRITERS IN THE WORLD

Writers of African heritage have been heralded in many countries. Alexander Pushkin in Russia, Alexander Dumas and Aimé Cesaire in France, Langston Hughes and Toni Morrison in the United States, and Nicolas Guillen in Cuba have demonstrated enormous capacities in language and culture. Have students research these names and report on them in class. Identify qualities of character, discipline, and hard work and emphasize this to the class. This list is not complete but each teacher can add to the list from African and African American history books. There are books on inventors, astronauts, and the Egyptian philosophers. Most of the Egyptian philosophers lived before the Greeks and achieved lasting recognition in Greece because the Greeks like Thales, Anaxagoras, Plato, Eudoxos, Anaxamander, Isocrates and Pythagoras went to school in Africa. Pythagoras spent 22 years in Egypt. Africans called the land Kemet and later the Greeks referred to it as Egypt.

CORRECTING WHAT'S WRONG IN EDUCATION

- There is something wrong with a society that does not teach students how to understand their past.
- There is something wrong with an education that causes the oppressed to imitate their oppressors in values and narratives.
- There is something wrong with a society that cannot overcome the ignorance of racism even when people are educated in its schools.

I do not advocate the position that the past was better than the future, nor am I encouraging teachers to live in the past. I simply suggest that studying the past allows us to choose what was good and to avoid what was bad in the past. African pedagogy from the time of the Mystery Schools in Egypt to the current schools where children learn by doing was grounded in spiritual values. The question of education was, "How does one become a good person?" Or in some societies, "How does one become human?" These are not considered relevant questions in education today and consequently we see that children who go through the American system often end up narcissistic and materialistic. African pedagogy was involved in socialization of the child; in the West the socialization of the child is left to other institutions, some social and some religious.

As soon as a woman became pregnant in many African societies the entire village began the process of education of prenatal socialization. Once the infant is born the village participates in the post-natal socialization process. Nothing is left to chance. The aim was the intense bonding of the mother and child so that everyone knows what is to be expected and what is to be done. Reciprocity is considered part of the process of learning in community and certain spaces are set-aside for this type of ritual. The child grows up in a community where all people are for him and he is for all people. These spaces are designated at times as sacred places. While one cannot repeat or imitate all of the bonding of a mother and a child in revolutionary pedagogy we suggest that the teacher becomes someone who discovers places or times or both that are special, sacred in other words, for the students. It might be the library or a table in the back of the classroom. This is not a space for punishment but for reflections, recovery or reading. My eighth grade teacher, Mrs. Austin would let me spend time in the library reading for thirty minutes if she wanted to make a point about me having done exceptionally well in class. I truly appreciated that recognition and time. She would often stop in to see that I was reading. Students remember those occasions and will work hard to keep that bonding. We call these rituals for a reason. They are not like other moments or spaces because they had these qualities:

- Shared Knowledge
- Shared Symbols
- Reinforced Social Bonds

- Used Art, Music, Reading
- Employed Games if Possible to Integrate Knowledge
- Celebrated in a Way that Allowed the Community to Mark Distinction

Engaging in this type of revolutionary pedagogy will help us to break the sieves through which urban children pass into the stream of negativity. Among these negative sieves used as crippling tools against African American children are special education, compensatory education, boot camp for violent children, vouchers and choice for the affluent to abandon the public schools, and direct instruction for poor and low achieving students. The revolutionary pedagogist insists on removing these stresses on the education experience by teaching children with a new pedagogy that recognizes and honors their agency to assert themselves while demonstrating an anti-racist ethic.

CHAPTER SIX

Revolutionary Illustrations And Demonstrations

Joyce E. King says, "Critical, transformative teachers must develop a pedagogy of social action and advocacy that really celebrates diversity, not just random holidays, isolated cultural artifacts, or "festivals and food" (King, 1991 p. 134). In this assessment King is following Bill Ayers argument in his article, "Young Children and the Problem of the Color Line" in *Democracy and Education*. (Ayers, 1988, pp. 20-26). Ayers, a prominent educator, contends that the public school system is much too rigid and hostile toward creativity and much too bureaucratic and too rigid for effective education. In Ayers' mind the educational system normally structures learning in ways that prevent independent thinking. Ayers has campaigned for years to secure respect for the individual growth of each student. Like the revolutionary pedagogists, Ayers questions the classifications of students based on standardized tests rather than on human creativity, thus encouraging and supporting a transformed philosophy in education.

Both King and Ayers occupy key positions in the progressive ranks of educators who seek to extend democracy in school systems. They understand the need for illustrative and demonstrative materials to assist teachers in getting up to speed in the revolutionary pedagogy.

I will present here a number of illustrative and demonstrative examples that might be used in explaining and interpreting facts, themes, conditions, environments, and personalities in education. An illustration is an example used to clarify something that is often accompanied by an image or picture. A demonstration is an act of providing evidence to show the truth of a certain idea, argument, or concept. It may or may not be augmented by an illustration. If we are to improve the dissemination of knowledge and the distribution of democracy in education we must also create opportunities for revolutionary pedagogy by giving the teachers the best tools possible.

My aim here is to show teachers who want to be revolutionary pedagogists how and what to use to establish a mode of instruction that would re-center dislocated African American students and expand the knowledge of all other students in the classroom. Here are a few themes and pedagogical scaffolds that will assist the teacher seeking to reason ways to approach important topics.

The Enslavement of Africans In America

The teaching of the enslavement has been one of the most difficult areas for teachers to cover adequately. In Revolutionary Pedagogy the teacher must become an active participant in raising the consciousness of students about the horrors and evils of the enslavement. So how do you teach about the enslavement of Africans? One must do it, as one would teach about the Holocaust. Those who created the institution of chattel slavery, like those who created the conditions for the Holocaust, did so out of a belief that the victims were less than the perpetrators in terms of human value. The Enslavement of Africans was a crime against humanity and can never be supported in any way. There are no silver or gold linings in the inimical clouds of depravity that produced the horrendous bondage of millions of people.

Since we have few written records by Africans during the enslavement, how do we teach about the enslavement? The revolutionary pedagogist must use what is available. For example, we know that announcements of runaways were common because Africans ran away from the plantations and farms quite regularly. Whites placed advertisements in newspapers seeking to have whites in the public capture and return Africans to enslavement. Those ads can become primary evidence about the lifestyles, dress, attitudes, histories, courage, families, and intelligence of Africans. For example in the newspaper ads below I have followed each one with questions that might be discussed, descriptions that might be investigated, and attitudes that might demonstrate the state of mind of Africans in resistance to enslavement.

Using 18ᵀᴴ Century Runaway African Advertisements as Heuristic Examples for Understanding Africans

May 5, 1738. Ran away from the Subscriber's Quarters on Sapponic, in Prince George County, 14 or 15 Weeks ago, a Mulattoe Man Slave, named Tom, 25 Years old, about 5 feet 8 or 9 Inches high, thin faced, and bushy Hair, if not cut off; he is very apt to grin when he speaks, or is spoken to; had on an old dark Fustian Coat, with plain yellow Metal Buttons; Hath been several Times taken up, and escaped again before he could be deliver'd to the Quarter whereunto he belon'd; and the last Time shackled, Handcuffed, and an Iron Collar about his Neck, with Prongs, and to some of them Links. Whoever will deliver him to me, in Charles-City County, shall have a Pistole Reward, besides what the law allows; and if brought from any great Distance a farther Reward suitable to the Trouble, by *John Stith.*

N.B. It is suspected he will endeavour to escape on Board some Vessel.

Questions

1. What is a mulatto? What are the origins of mulatto populations during slavery?
2. What is a "Fustian Coat"? How would an enslaved person have gotten such a coat?
3. The fact that Tom had escaped and been captured several times before, including "the last Time shackled, Handcuffed, and an Iron Collar about his Neck, with Prongs, and to some of them Links" what do you think was his attitude about his bondage?
4. What does it say about Tom's intelligence that he might "endeavor" to escape on board a boat?

May 2, 1766. Run away from the subscriber, in Mecklenburg county on Wednesday last, a fellow named Jack. It appears he has been principally concerned in promoting the late disorderly meetings among the Negroes, and is gone off for fear of being prosecuted for many robberies he has committed. He is a low squat made fellow, bow-legged, his eyes remarkably red, has been branded on the right cheek R, and on the left M, though not easily to be perceived. It is supposed he intends for Carolina or Georgia. Whoever apprehends the said slave, and will deliver him to me, shall receive 50s. If taken 50 miles from home and 6d [pence] a mile for a greater distance. ***Robert Munford.***

Questions

1. What does it say about Jack's courage that "It appears he has been principally concerned in promoting the late disorderly meetings among the Negroes""
2. What would be considered "disorderly meetings" in your judgment? Discuss this with the students.
3. What "robberies" by Jack would be greater than his escape, which is the taking of "property" from the slaveholder? Discuss the idea of chattel slavery.
4. Find out how much 50 shillings would have been during this period.
5. Speak about his physical traits and the branding on his face. Explain the idea of branding of enslaved Africans.

Oct. 10, 1767. Prince George, Sept. 28, 1767. RUN away from the subscriber, the 22d of this instant, three slaves, viz. JUPITER, alias GIBB, a Negro fellow, about 35 years of age, about 6 feet high, knock kneed, flat footed, the right knee bent in more than the left, has several scars on his back from a severe whipping he lately had at Sussex court-house, having been tried there for stirring up the Negroes to an insurrection, being a great Newlight preacher. ROBIN about 25 years of age, a stout fellow, about 6 feet high, has a film over one of his eyes, a sore on one of his shins, and is brother to Gibb. DINAH, an old wench, very large, near 6 feet high; she has a remarkable stump of a thumb, occasioned by a whitlow, by which the bones of the first joint came out and is mother to the two fellows. They carried with them a variety of clothes, among the rest an old blue duffil great coat, one bearskin do. a scarlet jacket, and a fine new linen shirt. It is supposed they will endeavour to make their escape southward. Whoever takes up, and conveys to me the above slave, shall have a reward of 50s. for each of the fellows, and 20s for the wench, if taken in Virginia; if any other government, £5 for each of the fellows, and 40s for the wench paid by *George Noble.*

Questions

1. What does it say about planning that three enslaved Africans were able to escape at the same time?
2. Explain the relationship between Jupiter, Robin and Dinah. Discuss the significance of mother and sons running away together.
3. How could the "severe whipping" had affected Jupiter's willingness to escape?
4. What does it say about Jupiter that he had a role in "stirrig up the Negroes to an insurrection"?

Oct. 20, 1768. RUN away from the subscriber in Chesterfield, the Wednesday before Easter last, a bright mulatto wench named Jude, about 30 years old is very remarkable, has lost one eye, but which I have forgot, has long black hair, a large scar on one of her elbows, and several other scars on her face, and has been subject to running away ever since she was ten years old. I have great reason to think she will pass for a free woman, and endeavour to make into South Carolina. She is very knowing about house business, can spin, weave, sew, and iron, well. She had on when she went away her winter clothing, also a blue and white striped Virginia cloth gown, a Virginia cloth coperas and white striped coat, besides others too tedious to mention. Whoever conveys the said slave to me shall be well rewarded for their trouble. *Mary Clay.*

Questions

1. What may have been Jude's calculation to leave just before Easter?
2. What was her physical condition? Speculate on how she may have gotten the scars on her body, the lost eye and the scar on her elbow.
3. Why could she pass as a free woman?
4. Explain how her knowledge "about house business" could indicate intelligence and could provide her skills to escape and live on her own.

May 11, 1769. Run away from the subscriber in Charles City county, the 14th of April last, a VIRGINIA born Negro fellow named PETER, about 44 years of age, of a black complexion, a slim fellow, his teeth cut before as if broke off, and is a sly artful rogue if not watched; he carried with him sundry clothes, such as crop Negroes usually wear, also a white Virginia cloth waistcoat and petticoat, a Tarlton plaid gown, and sundry other of his wife's clothes. He also carried away a gun of an uncommon large size, and a fiddle, which he is much delighted in when he gets any strong drink, which he is remarkably fond of, and then very talkative and impudent. I suspect he has gone to Amelia county, to

Mr. Tanner's, as Mrs. Tanner, alias Mrs. Johnson, sold him to Mr. Richard Hayles, and by him sold to the subscriber, as he often told the other Negroes that if ever I used him ill he would go to his old mistress, as she never sold him to Mr. Hayles, but only lent him during pleasure, and that he would go to her and be protected. The said Negro is outlawed; and I will give £10 to any person or persons that will kill him and bring me his head, separate from his body, or 40s. if delivered to the subscriber near the Long Bridge. *William Gregory.*

Questions

1. Why is Peter considered "a sly artful rogue if not watched"?
2. Explain how those who "stole" him or his ancestors into slavery are not considered "rogues" but the man who escapes is considered such a bad person?
3. Explain Tarlton plaid gown.
4. What are the implications of Peter having a gun? What would the gun be used for?

Oct. 13, 1774. Run away from the Subscriber, last Friday, a likely Virginia born Negro Man called JOHNNY, about 22 Years of Age, five Feet eight Inches high, has a down Look, and Waiter. This Fellow formerly belonged to Armistead Lightfoot, Esq; deceased, and is remarkable for Cock-fighting, Card-playing, and many other Games. I suspect he will pass as a Freeman, and endeavour to get out of the Colony, as he can read and write. All Masters of Vessels are cautioned not to carry him off, at their Peril. I will give 40s. if taken within this Colony and brought home, besides what the Law allows, or £5 if taken in any other Colony. *Charles Grymes.*

Questions

1. Discuss Johnny's physical condition.
2. Discuss Johnny's ability in organizing and conducting Cock-fighting, Card-playing, and many other Games. What gives Charles Grymes the idea that Johnny might try to appear as a freeman?

June 16, 1775. TEN POUNDS REWARD Run away from the subscriber in Dunmore county, in May last, a negro fellow named SAM. 5 feet 5 or 6 inches high, has a broad face, and is a well looking fellow. As to his clothing, I cannot be certain, he having carried several things with him. He also took with him an old bay horse very gray about the head, an iron pot, a narrow axe, a handsaw, and an old smooth bore gun. About three years ago he purchased his freedom of his old master, Mr. Francis Slaughter, and continued in that state till this spring, when it was discovered he was attempting to inveigle away a number of negroes to the new or Indian country (where he had been most of the last summer) upon which the neighbours insisted on his being reduced to slavery again, and I purchased him. I imagine he will endeavour to pass as a freeman, he having a discharge from his old master, as well as one from Lord Dunmore, having served in the expedition against the Indians last fall. Whoever delivers said slave to me shall have the reward that is offered. *Gabriel Jones.*

Questions

1. Describe Sam according to this ad and comment on the fact that the advertisement says "is a well looking fellow."
2. What does it mean that he was able to take an old bay horse, an iron pot, an axe, a handsaw, and a smooth bore gun? Does this suggest that he is skilled?

3.   Why would he be able to purchase his freedom three years earlier and then be re-enslaved?

4.   Claiming that Sam was attempting "to inveigle away a number of negroes to the new or Indian country", the ad suggests that he had been reduced to enslavement again. Please discuss Sam's situation as an individual seeking to free himself and others.

Dec. 1, 1774. RUN away from the subscriber in Dinwiddie, the 5th day of April last, a dark mulatto man named JEMMY, 5 feet 9 or 10 inches high, well made, has remarkable long feet, the middle toes longer than the rest, which they ride over, has lost part of one of his foreteeth, which occasions the next to it to look blue, is a very artful fellow, and will probably endeavour to pass for a freeman; he is very fond of singing hymns and preaching, and has been about Williamsburg ever since he went off, passing by the name of James Williams. Whoever apprehends the said slave, and secures him so that I get him again, shall have 40s reward, and if delivered to me in Dinwiddie L4. *David Walker.*

Questions

1.   What would be a "dark mulatto" man?

2.   Jemmy is said to be "well made" but there was evidence that he had lost one of his front teeth and had long feet. What does it mean that he was "an artful fellow"?

3.   Speculate on the possibility that this man may have passed for a freeman. How? Why?

4.   Jemmy was said to sing hymns and to preach, what does that say about the readiness of his mind to use all avenues for escape, including religion?

Nov. 29, 1776. RUN away the first of January 1775 a likely mulatto negro wench named Kate, 18 years of age, well made, 5 feet 9 or 10 inches high, and talks very smooth. She was hired to mr. Philip Moody of Williamsburg in 1774, and last year to mr. John Thruston, from whence she ran off. She has got a husband in Williamsburg, and probably may pass for a free person as she is well acquainted in that city, and I have repeatedly heard of her being there. She formerly belonged to the estate of Mr. John Cary, deceased, of York county. I will give 20s. to any person that will secure her in jail and give me intelligence thereof, or 40s if brought to me in King & Queen, at Mr. John Thruston's. *EDWARD CARY, jun.*

Questions

1. What is the meaning of "wench"? How was she "likely"?
2. How do we know that she was intelligent?
3. What does it say that she was passed from one slaveholder to another on three separate occasions?
4. Imagine what her life must have been and what may have finally driven her away.

RAN away from the subscriber, living on West river, on the 26th of October last, a very likely negro girl named PEGG, she is about fifteen years of age, very black and small for her age, speaks low when spoken to, has been used to wait in the house: had on when she went away an old blue cotton jacket and petticoat, but is probable she got other cloathing since her elopement. The above reward, including what the law allows, will be given to any person apprehending said girl, and securing her in any gaol, so that I get her again, or reasonable charges if brought home, by Gassaway Pindell.

Questions

1. What does this ad say about the age and gender of those running away?
2. Pegg was small and spoke in quiet tones but yet was able to plan her escape. What could have caused her desire to leave the employ of Gassaway Pindell?
3. What is the meaning of home in Pindell's ad?

URBAN TEACHERS AND DEAD WHITE MEN

Why Should White Philosophers be the Only Ones on the List

In the 21st century the vestiges of the racist elements of the Enlightenment must be abandoned and teachers, especially those taking up the cause of revolutionary pedagogy, must place a new critical eye on all white philosophers. One of the reasons there remains a need for revolutionary pedagogists is because the promotion of white philosophers is probably at the vanguard of all racist thinking. We will never rid the educational system of racism until we understand that Hegel, Voltaire, Locke, Montesquieu, and Thomas Jefferson buttressed the system.

Students at the University of London's School for Oriental and African Studies protested the teaching of white philosophers in January 2017. According to the London Telegraph writer Camilla Turner reporting on the students' demands said, "They say it is part of wider campaign to "decolonise" the university, as they seek to "address the structural and epistemological legacy of colonialism"(January 8, 2017). Teshale Tibebu argued in his classic study Hegel and the Third World that "Hegel, more than any other modern Western philosopher, produced the most systematic case for the superiority of Western white Protestant bourgeois modernity. He established a racially structured ladder of gradation of the peoples of the world, putting Germanic people at the top of the racial pyramid, people of Asia in the middle, and Africans and Indigenous people of the Americas and Pacific Islands at the bottom" (Tibebu, 2011). There is no wonder that the revolutionary pedagogist must see Hegel as the source of many of the ideas that have trickled down to the elementary and secondary systems of education. Hegel was not alone in his belief that Africans represented the lowest rung of humanity.

Of course, it should be noted that the venerated Thomas Jefferson is probably the person most responsible for advancing racist theories in the United States. He was not the first European to create notions of racial hierarchy but he was the first American to argue for the separation of the races. Jefferson claimed that "All men are created equal" yet the same person declared in *Notes on Virginia* that he was apt to believe with suspicion that blacks are inferior to whites in mind and body. Obviously one of the leading philosophers of the United States was a racist. How do you teach a Thomas Jefferson without teaching that a man who "owned" 200 other human beings is a disgrace to humanity? In the same vein, what does a revolutionary pedagogist say about George Washington who held more than 300 blacks in bondage?

CONCLUSION

A new topography of social existence in this diversely populated nation requires us to map out new pedagogical territories. What is at stake is our understanding of the importance of common historical conflicts over land between the Native Americans, for example, and how Africans have been viewed in this society during and since the enslavement. The idea of subjugation, that is, subjugation of fellow humans and nature, has to be seen as central to the pedagogy of capitalist societies. But subjugation was not just physically violent but culturally violent and in certain cases a form of cultural genocide.

Let me quickly add that this new topography depends upon the acceptance of our common humanity. The revolutionary pedagogist does not define others as evil, primitive, devils, and so forth in order to minimize them. Such name-calling and negative attitudes toward other people create the drama of human elimination, persecution, and hegemony. Negativity endures through all forms of post modernism and post colonialism because teachers who refuse to listen to the silences or to hear the emotion in others are doing nothing more than dictating a paradigm, however obsolete, while saying there is not paradigm.

The new topography also depends upon our identity, I mean, the acceptance of who we are as human beings. So we embrace our common humanity by accepting that we are human alongside others, not above others. Running away from one's own history and culture in order to drown oneself in anonymity/struggle is to rebuild our identity out of the embers of the fires of enslavement and colonialism.

I have written excitedly because all teaching is the recognition of the gifts that our students bring. I am richer because of my engagement with many students that I have had in classes over the decades. Indeed, I think that as a revolutionary pedagogist I have reached new heights of understanding because as the scientist, Neil deGrasse Tyson would say, "We are all star material from the same star system of the universe." As such we must be encounter and obliterate ignorance whenever and wherever we see it.

The revolutionary pedagogist leaps to end all forms of discrimination based on false premises of race, gender, religion, class, and fashion. That is why I contend that what the truly authentic revolutionary pedagogist sees is often different from what others see but we can learn to cross boundaries to the magic of knowing and acting on what we know. Nearly five thousand years ago the ancient African philosopher, Ptahhotep, stated that the standards of good speech by saying "A man teaches as he acts. The wise person feeds the soul with what endures, so that it is happy with person on earth. The wise is known by his good actions. The heart of the wise matches his or her tongue and hits or her lips are straight when he or she speaks. The wise have eyes that are made to see and ears that are made to hear what will profit children. The wise is a person who acts with Maat and is free of falsehood and disorder" (*The Teaching of Ptahhotep*).

References

Anderson, J. D. *The Education of Blacks in the South, 1860-1935.* Chapel Hill: University of North Carolina Press, 1988.

Arnez, Nancy *The Besieged School Superintendent.* University Press of America, l981.

Asante, Molefi K. "The Afrocentric Idea in Education," *Journal of Negro Education.* Volume 60, no. 2, 1991, pp. 170-180.

Asante, Molefi K. *The Afrocentric Idea.* Philadelphia: Temple University Press, l990

Asante, Molefi K. *Afrocentricity.* Chicago: AAI, 2003.

Ayers, Williams, "Young Children and the Problem of the Color Line" *Democracy and Education.* l988

Banks, James A. *Educating Citizens in a Multicultural Society* (New York: Teachers College Press, 2007

Barrows, Isabel C. *First Mohonk Conference on the Negro Question*, held at Lake Mohonk, Ulster County, New York, June 4, 5, 6, 1890, Boston: George Ellis Printer, 1890.

Berry, Henry, "The Abolition of Slavery," In *The Roving Editor: Or, Talks with Slaves in the Southern States* edited by James Redpath, 1859, pp. 100-102 as well as in 100-102. Originally published l831.

Bloom, Allan. *The Closing of the American Mind: How Education has Failed Democracy and Impoverished the Souls of Today's Students.* New York: Simon and Shuster, 2012.

Clarke, John Henrik, *My Life in Search of Africa.* Ithaca: Africana Research Center, 1994.

Dei, George Sefa, *Teaching Africa: Towards a Trangressive Pedagogy.* Toronto: Springer, 2010.

Emdin, Christopher. *For White Folks Who Teach in the Hood.* New York: Teachers College Press, 2015.

Ferreira, Ana Monteiro. *The Demise of the Inhuman.* Albany: SUNY Press, 2015.

Feldstein, Stanley, *Once a Slave: The Slaves' View of Slavery*. New York: William Morrow Company, 1971.

Goodwin, Susan. *Teacher Knowledge about Educating Children of African Descent in Urban Schools*. Doctoral Dissertation. St. John Fisher College, August 2010

Hilliard, Asa G. III, *SBA: The Reawakening of the African Mind*. Gainesville, Florida: Makare Publishers, 1998.

Hirsch, E. D., *Cultural Literacy. What Every American Needs to Know*. New York: Vintage, 1988.

James, George, *Stolen Legacy: Greek Philosophy is Stolen Egyptian Philosophy*. CreateSpace Independent Publishing Platform, 2014

Karenga, Maulana. *Kwanzaa: A Celebration of Family, Community and Culture*. Los Angeles: University of Sankore Press, 1997.

Karenga, Maulana. http://www.us-organization.org/30th/ppp.html

Karenga, Maulana, *Selections from the Husia: Sacred Wisdom from Ancient Egypt*. Los Angeles: University of Sankore Press, 1984. 2nd Edition.

Karenga, Maulana, "Libation for Limbiko Tembo," *Los Angeles Sentinel*, June 25, 2009.

Keto, C. Tsehloane, *The Africa Centered Perspective of History*. New Jersey: K and A Publishers, 1990.

King, Joyce E., "Dysconscious Racism: Ideology, Identity, and the Miseducation of Teachers" *The Journal of Negro Education*, Vol. 60, No. 2 (Spring, 1991), pp. 133-146

Kunjufu, Jawanza, *Countering the Conspiracy to Destroy Black Boys, Volume 1*. Chicago: AAI, 1985.

Kunjufu, Jawanza, *Keeping Black Boys Out of Special Education, Chicago: AAI, 2005.*

Ladson-Billings, Gloria, "Toward a Theory of Culturally Relevant Pedagogy" *American Educational Research Journal*, Vol. 32, No. 3. (Autumn, 1995), pp. 465-491

Mazama, Ama and Garvey Musumunu. *African Americans and Homeschooling: Motivations, Opportunities and Challenges*. New York: Routledge, 2014.

Miike, Y. (2007). Asian contributions to communication theory: An introduction. China Media Research, 3(4), 1-6.

Monderson, Fred. *Ladies in the House*. New York: SuMon, 2013

NCES (nces.ed.gov/pubs/web/96184ex.asp) *Race Against Time: Educating Black Boys* (February 2011, 2 MB, 8pp

Ptahhotep, *The Teaching of Ptahhotep*. See Molefi Kete Asante, *Egyptian Philosophers*. Chicago: African American Images.

Raju, C. K. *Is Science Western in Origin?* Dissenting Knowledges Pamphlet No. 8. New Delhi, 2012.

Reardon, Sean F. and Ximena A. Portilla, "Recent Trends in Income, Racial, and Ethnic School Readiness Gaps at Kindergarten Entry". *AERA Open*, July 1, 2016

Rivers, Freya A. *Swallowed Tears: A Memoir*. AuthorHouse, 2012.

Sousa Santos, Boaventura de, "Beyond Abyssal Thinking," *Eurozine*, 6, 29, 2007

Tibebu, Teshale, *Hegel and the Third World: The Making of Eurocentrism in World History*. Syracuse, New York: Syracuse University Press, 2011.

Woodson, Carter G. *The Mis-education of the Negro*. New York: Tribeca, 2013.

Yin, J., & Miike, Y., A textual analysis of fortune cookie sayings: How Chinese are they? *Howard Journal of Communications*, 2008, 19(1), 18-43.

Index

141

CPSIA information can be obtained
at www.ICGtesting.com
Printed in the USA
LVHW010202110720
660356LV00019B/685

9 780982 532744